1980

Classroom Practices in Teaching English 1977-1978

Teaching the Basics—Really!

NCTE Committee on Classroom Practices in Teaching English

Classroom Practices
in Teaching English
1977-1978

Teaching the Basics—
Really!

Ouida Clapp, Chair,
and the Committee on Classroom Practices

National Council of Teachers of English
1111 Kenyon Road, Urbana, Illinois 61801

Grateful acknowledgment is made for permission to reprint the following material. "A narrow fellow in the grass" is reprinted by permission by the publishers and the Trustees of Amherst College from THE POEMS OF EMILY DICKINSON, edited by Thomas H. Johnson, Cambridge, Mass.: The Belknap Press of Harvard University Press, Copyright © 1951, 1955 by the President and Fellows of Harvard College. "Pray in May" and "The Most Vital Thing in Life" are from LITERATURE: STRUCTURE, SOUND, AND SENSE by Laurence Perrine, © 1963, 1969 by Harcourt Brace Jovanovich, Inc. and reprinted with their permission.

Staff Editors: Carol Schanche and Kathy Roos
Cover Design: Tom Kovacs

NCTE Stock Number 06870

Library of Congress Cataloging in Publication Data

National Council of Teachers of English. Committee
    on Classroom Practices.
    Teaching the basics—really!

    (Classroom practices in teaching English ; 1977–1978)
    Includes bibliographies.
    1.   English language—Study and teaching—Addresses, essays, lectures.   2.   Language arts—Addresses, essays, lectures.   I.   Clapp, Ouida H.   II.   Title.   III.   Series.
LB1576.N285 1977   428'.007'1   77-21003
ISBN 0-8141-0687-0

Contents

Preface

The topic for this year's *Classroom Practices* was inescapable. In November 1976, in Chicago, the participants at the annual open meeting of the Committee on Classroom Practices in the Teaching of English debated the merits of several topics, but invariably the discussion returned to a stand on the "basics." This issue of *Classroom Practices*, we felt, must showcase the practices of English teachers across the country, practices which we recognize as everyday, carefully determined responses to our students' need to use language effectively and easily.

During the fall, winter, and into the spring, the call for manuscripts appeared in *Language Arts*, *English Journal*, and *College English*, as well as in newsletters and journals of many NCTE affiliates and in various subject-related publications. Seventy-one manuscripts from twenty-four states arrived for the committee's consideration. Committee members Jeffrey Golub, Sandra Seale, Gene Stanford, and Raymond Rodrigues assisted the editor in reading and evaluating the material submitted by classroom teachers of English, speech, and reading; curriculum coordinators and supervisors; department chairs; program directors; a librarian; an elementary school principal; and a college dean.

The book, given its name by the participants at the November meeting, is organized in six sections, each devoted to a language skill. Not surprisingly, in view of the fact that the NCTE Secondary Section declared this a "Year of Composition," a large number of the articles address that topic.

This issue, like its predecessors, is an interesting reflection of the collective mind and temperament of outstanding teachers of English. The committee believes that *Teaching the Basics—Really!* will be a valuable source of ideas for language arts instruction.

Introduction

"Teaching the Basics—Really!" is exactly what we're doing, and doing better now than ever before! This is the assertion made by this issue of *Classroom Practices in the Teaching of English*.

Teachers of English language arts know what "the basics" are and, contrary to some well-intentioned but uninformed critics, have not failed to give the basics an appropriate place and emphasis in the English language arts curriculum. Reading, writing, speaking, understanding and appreciating language are central to our discipline. And with a constantly developing command of these basic skills, our students will be able to proceed with confidence to discover and communicate their views on subjects important to them. These students will acquire a minimum competence, to use currently popular jargon, in the skills that a literate society requires of those who would be fully participating members.

The often strident demand to "return to the basics" arises generally from a feeling that we as a society are failing to cope with our problems. It represents a simplistic solution that is neither novel nor, in view of the attraction nostalgia holds, surprising. For many adults, the world of their youth was a happier time and place. Problems existed in those days, but they were not overwhelming. What memories remain of elementary and secondary school days are largely pleasant. From their language arts instruction, adults remember Tom Sawyer, Silas Marner, and the Headless Horseman. Some can still recite the opening lines of a *Hamlet* soliloquy and will do so at the slightest provocation. They remember the spelling tests and the drills on nouns, verbs, adjectives, and adverbs. The parts of speech were undoubtedly of major importance because teachers taught them over and over year after year. Not so well remembered is the time spent writing letters, poems, and compositions. As a consequence of their less-than-complete memories, many adults are persuaded that their writing skills stem from the time they spent learning agreement of subject and verb and in practicing sentence diagramming.

Such recollections notwithstanding, the fact is that whatever mastery in writing was achieved came about as a result of the student's "languaging" often, and in the process learning to recognize the power of language and to respect its system and order.

Experience has shown that the greater the activity with language, the better and more lasting the results. The classroom practices submitted for this publication clearly show language arts teachers hold this conviction, which can be buttressed with the findings of some thirty years of linguistic scholarship and with the wealth of recent research about composition. Understanding the writing process more fully enables us to teach basic skills with greater success.

The teaching of English transcends the penmanship, spelling, and grammar emphasized in arguments about the basics. Those are important skills which should be and are being taught. But they are not enough and must not be taught in isolation. Along with listening, speaking, reading, writing, and appreciating literature, they must be taught in contexts that guarantee a continuous reinforcement of each skill by the others. English teachers have not lost faith or abandoned instruction in the basic communication skills. Rather, they have drawn strength from the knowledge that "language is a communication process, and that the whole of communication is much greater than the sum of its parts," as the SLATE Steering Committee explained in its August 1976 bulletin, *What Are the Basics in English?*

The purpose of this book is not to put English teachers on the road back to the basics, for that road has always been well traveled. But we hope that this collection will provide some fresh approaches, and new insights to make that road less bumpy.

Ouida H. Clapp

1 About Teaching Reading

Of the "three Rs," reading may be the most basic of all. But basic certainly doesn't mean simple. Reading is a highly complex process involving innumerable skills. Helpful classroom ideas for strengthening some of these skills in our students are offered in this chapter. Articles endorsing early emphasis on critical reading skills, developing an ability to pick out key words, using a cloze procedure to encourage use of context cues, and presenting exercises to clarify transitional language all work to develop necessary skills in reading. Finally, an assessment-prescriptive model for use with college students is provided.

The business of teaching reading is as complex as the reading process itself. These ideas are meant to make that teaching more effective.

Three Elements of Critical Reading

Arthur E. Smith, State University College at Brockport

Critical reading is often placed at the upper end of reading skill hierarchies. This suggests that the skills of critical reading can be mastered only after a reader is fully proficient at several levels of preceding skills. However, instruction in critical reading need not be delayed until a student shows complete mastery of "earlier" reading skills. In fact, it is not only possible to teach critical reading at an early level, it is absolutely imperative. The ability to read critically is of paramount importance in a democratic society where there is open competition for people's opinions and beliefs. Indeed, critical reading is basic to survival in our society.

Critical reading broadly refers to those aspects of comprehension which involve the reader in an assessment of the author's intent and a recognition of the devices used by writers to influence the reader. The following suggestions are intended to introduce critical reading skills at the intermediate/middle school level. Critical analysis of the printed word in advertising is emphasized.

Word Selection

One simple technique which can help readers to look at advertisements more critically is to omit modifiers while reading advertising copy. Phrases such as "race-car precision" and "luxurious comfort" appear less impressive and more realistic when the adjectives are deleted. A variation of the advertisement is the restaurant menu. A class might examine several menus from local restaurants and then create their own menu which would "garnish" the offerings from the school cafeteria.

Readers also need to be aware that advertisers frequently capitalize on the connotative meanings of words to influence the public. Why does the real estate ad refer to a "home" rather than a "house"? How do pairs such as "slender/thin" or "vagabond/tramp" differ in their suggested meanings? Most youngsters are familiar with the names of automobile models; students could be asked to examine the reasons that Detroit spends hundreds of thousands of dollars to come up with names like Cobra, Cougar, Monte Carlo, or Aspen. What other animal or place names can students list which might suggest those qualities that an auto manufacturer would want to project?

Use of Statistics

While statistics can be studied to an advanced level, there are also some basic considerations with which the developing reader can begin. One of these is the difference between "median" and "mean" as types of averages. An eager young schoolchild, responding to a magazine ad for door-to-door sales work, might be impressed by the statement that "Last summer, the average student salesperson earned $500." This could be a misleading "average" including the one exceptional person who earned $4,000 and all the others who earned closer to $50 each.

Another method of manipulating statistics is to present figures on a graph which looks favorable to the advertiser's position. For instance, an advertisement for a pain-relief remedy may display a graph suggesting a dramatic drop in the number of headaches within hours of taking the medicine. The implication is that the medicine effects the relief. Not shown would be a graph plotting headache relief among people taking no medication. This graph might be an embarrassment to the advertiser if it closely paralleled the printed graph, suggesting that no treatment at all appeared to be as effective as medication in reducing pain.

For the teacher of a self-contained class, this element of critical reading offers an opportunity to integrate the studies of language and math. Students can quickly see how these disciplines can help them in the "real world." Sets of data and hypothetical situations can be given to students who then decide the fairest way to present the information and how that same information might appear in an advertisement.

Fact/Opinion Distinction

Another major skill of critical reading is distinguishing fact from opinion. The consumer must decide which of the many "statements of fact" appearing in advertising copy are truly factual and which reflect the opinions of the advertiser. The teacher might display a full-page color ad from a national magazine which proclaims a particular auto to be "the quietest riding car in America." How do we know? Because the manufacturer says so? Because Kevin's father drives one and he says so? A discussion will easily develop about sources of information and objectivity. The investigation might be continued as students write to the manufacturer for supporting evidence. Government agencies and independent consumer groups might also be contacted and their replies compared.

At other times, students may do their own research to test the statements made in advertisements. Brands X and Y of paper towels can be carefully checked for their "wet strength." Parallel patches of linoleum tile can be treated with two different brands of floor wax and observed for deterioration of the shine. A cluster of other skills, including planning, observation, and record keeping, would be involved in such activities.

Even valid studies are often used to suggest conclusions which do not necessarily follow from the research results. Consider the statement, "Our cigarette has been shown to be lowest in tar and nicotine of any cigarette on the market today." Assuming for the moment the truth of that statement, the reader must be taught to look beyond it and ask, "What does this ad imply?" The manufacturer hopes the ad will convince the readers that the cigarette is not harmful to their health. Certainly such an extrapolation from the facts could not be justified.

There are other elements to be considered in critical reading, but word selection, use of statistics, and fact/opinion distinction are three that can be easily used to introduce students to methods of manipulation employed by advertisers. Such an introduction actively involves students in their own learning as they seek out advertisements which exemplify certain techniques. These examples can be labeled and displayed in the classroom. As a further step toward active involvement, students can create their own ads using the manipulation techniques they have been studying. These ads could then be shared with classmates who would try to identify the technique used. These activities should help to develop some of the basic skills critical to an informed consumer.

References

Atwood, Beth S. *Developing Skills in Critical Reading*. Palo Alto, Calif.: Education Today Co., 1975.

Huff, Darrell. *How to Lie with Statistics*. New York: W. W. Norton & Co., 1954.

Potter, Robert R. *Making Sense*. New York: Globe Book Co., 1974.

Roden, Philip. *The Elusive Truth*. Glenview, Ill.: Scott, Foresman & Co., 1973.

Structuring Comprehension with Key Words

Thomas P. Fitzgerald, State Education Department, Albany, New York

Philip M. Connors, John F. Kennedy Junior High School, Enfield, Connecticut

We have all encountered students who are able to read words but do not seem to understand the content of what they read. We ask ourselves what techniques we might use to improve the reading comprehension of these students.

One basic element in the comprehension process is the attending behavior of the reader. A student may be skilled in decoding but still be unable to process the flow of language. Language arts teachers can translate these concerns into instructional questions. Are the students aware of the available cue systems in language: orthographic, syntactic, and semantic? Are they using these cues to assist their processing of information? What techniques might be employed to help develop these skills?

Comprehending information is an active process in which the reader decodes a message and then encodes it into memory. Usually the printed message and the encoded message do not have a one-to-one relationship. Rather, the reader identifies the semantic intent of the printed message and stores that information. One strategy which has encouraged students to process actively while reading is to have them recast the printed message into a second form. Outlining, summarizing, identifying key words, and structuring overviews are examples of recasting.

This article focuses on the recasting techniques of key words and structured overviews. Students are asked to identify what they perceive to be the essential words in a message unit, whether a sentence, paragraph, or selection from literature. This technique encourages the reader to process actively, to recast the information, and to utilize the language cues inherent in the message unit.

Students may be introduced to this procedure through a discussion of the core sentence related to both syntax and semantics. The selection of words, the order of sentences for emphasis, and the redundancy of language should be analyzed. Students may then generate a list of criteria defining key words at the sentence level, such as: (1) critical to the meaning of the sentence, (2) related to sentence core, and (3) difficult to predict from context. At the paragraph level, one additional criterion may be stipulated: that the key words, when linked, indicate the paragraph development.

This explication of the key word technique should be followed by an introduction to structured overviews emphasizing the relationship existing among the key words. Each student should practice both of these techniques, and then (1) tabulate selected key words, (2) discuss what words are "key" to the meaning of the message, and (3) analyze relationships through the use of structured overviews.

The versatility of these techniques is highlighted if we review their use at different levels. Selecting key words is directly affected by the complexity of the sentence. Examine the following two sentences and select those words you feel represent key words according to the three-part definition previously discussed.

1. My immigrant father moved to Brooklyn in search of a job.
2. Maryann endured a long, painful recovery, and she feared the day she would have to report back to work.

Based on the parameters set by the definition, students might select as keys such structural words as *father*, *moved*, and *Maryann*, *endured*, *feared*. They might recognize as key words the agent and results (i.e., *father*, *Brooklyn*, *job* and *Maryann*, *recovery*, *feared*) indicating the embedded thoughts in these sentences. Obviously no answer is wrong but each selection has a degree of "rightness"; some reveal a higher development of language awareness. Choosing words such as *my*, *moved*, and *search* from the first sentence reveals a misreading of its core message.

The discussion following the selection process provides an exchange of ideas as to why certain words "key" the central meaning of the sentence. Here, the teacher draws attention to the syntactic and semantic cues: core parts, clauses, and words selected and sentence order arranged by the writer. By rearranging the first sentence, the emphasis or meaning of the sentence is altered.

In search of a job, my immigrant father moved to Brooklyn.

As an immigrant, my father moved to Brooklyn in search of a job.

Moving to Brooklyn, my immigrant father searched for a job.

At the paragraph level, students are asked to select the key words and arrange them in a structured overview to demonstrate the relationship among them. Students may design their own structure to match the organization and development of the selection read or may employ one of the four formats provided. Students using key words in a structured overview are actively processing the message and attending to language cues.

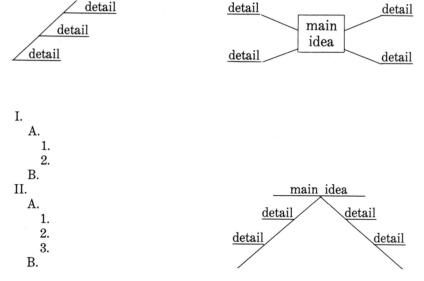

Fig. 1. Sample formats for analyzing paragraph structure.

The flexibility of this basic technique allows the teacher to focus on selecting key words related to such language arts skills as: (1) character development, (2) story development (plot, setting, tone), (3) author's purpose in writing, (4) specific organization (main idea, focus, detail), and (5) embedded thought in sentences. Here, the teacher directs the students to select those words which key the meaning or development in one of these areas, rather than the entire selection.

The techniques of key words and structured overviews, by setting a purpose for reading, prompting the use of language cues, and recognizing relationships between words and sentences, help students to more actively process and understand what they read. Selecting key words and recasting them in a structured overview permits wide application by teachers, while requiring little initial training for students.

Filling in the Blanks: Using the Cloze Procedure for Teaching Basic Skills

Douglas A. Tomas, University of Houston
Thomas Newkirk, University of New Hampshire

A *New Yorker* cartoon shows a man sitting in a downtown plaza staring at the tall building across from him. At first glance there appears to be nothing special about this scene, but a second look reveals a huge gorilla trapped inside the building. In a sense, we complete the picture of the building based on our expectations and a few bits of visual information only to find out a split second later that we have been fooled. The act of reconstructing a whole on the basis of parts and expectations is a natural human activity, one that is crucial in the reading process. F-r -x-mpl-, - th-nk y-- w-ll h-v- l-ttl- d-ff-c-lt- r--d-ng th-s -v-n th--gh th-r- -r- n- v-w-ls.

The cloze technique has been well validated as a means of assessing reading level (Rankin 1969). Briefly, students are given a passage in which every nth (5th, 10th, 20th, etc.) word is deleted until there is a total of about fifty-five blanks. Students then fill in the blanks with the words they "guess" were deleted. In scoring, the teacher counts only exact replacements. Synonyms are not counted because the percentages allow for even the good reader to make a number of inexact replacements. Also, scoring is made easier since the teacher does not have to determine the adequacy of a synonym. Students who fill in 61% or more of the blanks are reading at the "independent" level; they can read the material without teacher assistance. Students replacing 41–60% correctly are reading at the "instructional" level; they can read the passage, but may need some prereading assistance in areas such as vocabulary. Those students scoring less than 40% are reading at the "frustrational" level; the material is simply too difficult for them.

This means of assessment has been shown to correlate highly with standardized reading tests. The cloze tests can be easily constructed and scored by the classroom teacher. The technique is

10

far less time-consuming than administering either standardized tests or individual oral reading inventories. Most importantly, it is flexible; the teacher can use this technique on different days using different types of reading material.

Considerably less emphasis has been placed on using the cloze procedure for purely instructional purposes. Research has shown that simply having students fill in cloze blanks does not improve reading comprehension, and it is not difficult to imagine how tedious this could become after a while. But there are other classroom uses for the cloze procedure; some suggestions follow.

Closure and Word Attack

One implication of the work with cloze is that teachers should encourage students to use context clues to attack unknown words. Methods of word attack are: (1) context—using the language around a word to determine meaning; (2) structural analysis—breaking a word into parts (prefixes, root words, suffixes) and dividing compound words; (3) configuration clues—clues derived from word shape; (4) phonic analysis—transforming the written symbols into sounds and combining the sounds into recognizable words; and (5) dictionary use—looking up unknown words. There is little point in taking a dogmatic position and claiming that one of these is totally sufficient. However, it can be argued that context clues, which draw upon students' oral-aural language ability, should be the first means of word attack. Patterns of language use that students have heard and spoken may help them guess at an unknown word. On a more basic level, after the age of five, children have mastered most of the syntactic rules of the language; this gives them a tremendous tool for word attack. For example, "I *scrogged* Bill in the mouth." The student already has a pretty good idea of what *scrogged* means. It is a verb, something that "I" did. Not only is it a verb but it is an active verb implying physical contact. The next sentence might give Bill's reaction to being scrogged and narrow this meaning down even further. In this case, to go on to other means of word attack would probably be pointless.

When students have trouble with a word, instead of asking them to sound it out or to look for smaller words in the larger word, the teacher might ask "What do you think it means?" Have them finish the sentence and come back to the word. If this is of no help, either encourage students to go on to other means of word attack or to give the word a tentative meaning and then go on. This process has been called the "psycholinguistic guessing game," a term which perhaps overemphasizes the element of imprecision. A more apt metaphor might be the "reader as gambler." The gambler must determine when it is worthwhile to take a risk and when it would be better to play it safe. The seasoned gambler will argue that to play it safe is to take a risk of sorts. The reader can choose to play it safe by not leaving a word until it has been mastered, or to take a risk by giving a word a tentative meaning and then going on. The danger in playing it safe is that repeated interruptions can cause the sense of a passage to be lost; the danger of the second approach is that too many important words may be imprecisely determined. So the student must gamble. How can he become a good gambler? How can she be taught to be confident in her own inherent powers of word attack? How do teachers create an atmosphere in which readers are willing to take risks? The answer to each of these questions is through instructional use of the cloze procedure.

In this connection it is appropriate to say a few words about dictionary skills. In many English classes, students are encouraged to look up in the dictionary any word in their reading which they do not know. There is a rigor in this method that satisfies the puritan in all of us. But back to the odds. Virtually all formulas for word recognition assume that a reader can miss three to five words per one hundred and still read without a teacher's assistance. What is the price to be paid for sending students to the dictionary to try to fit one of several general meanings into a specific context, a process more difficult than often assumed? What does this do to reading enjoyment? What price in reading comprehension is paid for these periodic interruptions?

The great French essayist Montaigne, writing 400 years ago, said of his reading habits:

> When I meet with difficulties in my reading, I do not bite my nails over them; after making one or two attempts I give them up. If I were to sit down to them, I should be wasting myself and my time; my mind works at the first leap. What I do not see immediately, I see even less by persisting. Without lightness I achieve nothing; application and over-serious effort confuse, depress, and weary my brain.

This approach to reading, although certainly not new, is supported by recent research in psycholinguistics.

Different Types of Context Clues

Not only should students be encouraged to use context clues in the cloze procedure, but they should be encouraged to try to explain what clues they are using. Researchers have identified thirteen to fifteen different types of context clues that are helpful in word attack. While it would be cumbersome to deal with all of these, students should be aware of the more important types. One recent study (Tomas 1977) found that 50% of the correct cloze replacements relied on three types of context clues. Instruction might focus on these.

The first type is "clues derived from language experience and familiar expressions" and can be illustrated by: "No one would think he'd _____ such a beautiful corpse." Here the student might "guess" the word *make* because it completes a familiar expression.

The second type is termed "clues provided through repetition of words or the use of synonyms." Obviously there is little difficulty in identifying a word that has been identified before, but often there are synonyms or near synonyms that can provide clues to an unknown word: "He was hit by a *lacerating* blow to the cheek. A cut opened and began to drip blood." Here it is clear that a *lacerating* blow is one that could open a cut. The student might assume that *lacerating* means *cutting*. Note that here the significant clue came in the next sentence. This underlines the need for students not to stop dead when they come to an unknown word.

The third type of context clue is called "association clues." Here the mention of one object or concept calls forth an associated object or concept: "The AMA journal states that brutal punishment by parents is likely to be a 'more frequent cause of death than such well recognized diseases as leukemias, cystic fibrosis, and _____ dystrophy.'" Here one naturally associates the adjective *muscular* with *dystrophy*.

It is important to have students verbalize their reasons for certain choices. They should be consciously aware of closure strategies. Unlike the cloze assessment test where inexact replacements are counted wrong, both exact and approximate substitutions should be discussed. The why of substitution is more important than the what.

Closure and an Examination of Writing Style

Imagine, if you will, a passage in which every fifth word is deleted for a cloze test, and imagine that you can replace correctly every deleted word. Stylistically, the passage would surely be the dullest imaginable. In style, as in friends, absolute predictability is deadly. While readers rely on prediction, or context clues, in all types of reading, expectations occasionally need to be violated. In some types of writing this "surprise" element is more important than in others. Novelist Ford Maddox Ford has written that "carefully examined, a good—an interesting—style will consist of a constant succession of tiny, unobservable surprises." Mark Twain, in a similar vein, has commented on the importance of the author's choice of the "right word" as opposed to the "almost right" or expected word. "The difference between the almost right word and the right word is really a large matter— 'tis the difference between the lightning bug and the lightning."[1]

Tomas (1977), in a study of the use of closure in literary discourse, has shown that while closure was helpful in reading discourse, the percentage of correct replacements was below that expected. Graduate students in English were asked to replace words in complete literary selections, many of which were drawn from high school literature texts. The normal figure for successful replacements at the independent level (and one would expect the subjects to read this material at that level) is 61%. On only two of the five prose passages were the percentages above this figure; the average was 53.5%. But on the poetry selections, the average was 32%. The evidence suggests that it might be possible to use closure to study the surprise element in literary style.

An author can violate expectations in two major ways: by shifting syntax, or by choosing a particular word that would not be expected. We will focus on the second type of surprise here. Closure can be used to examine diction. One way in which this might be done is for the teacher to delete a particularly surprising word choice in a piece of prose or poetry and have the students guess the word. Invariably they will guess "the almost right word," which could lead to a discussion of the difference between the author's choice and the students' substitutions. Two possibilities are: "There is no *deodorant* like success." (Elizabeth Taylor)

---

1. An especially good chapter on literary style can be found in John Trimble's *Writing with Style* (Englewood Cliffs, N.J.: Prentice-Hall, 1975).

and "Many American parents have voiced the opinion that today's colleges are veritable breeding grounds for premarital sex. Nonsense. Each year literally *tens* of students graduate with their virtue intact." A third example might be Emily Dickinson's poem, "A narrow fellow in the grass," which contains what may be one of the most electric word choices in American literature (italics mine).

> Several of Nature's People
> I know, and they know me—
> I feel for them a transport
> Of cordiality—
>
> But never met this Fellow
> Attended, or alone
> Without a tighter breathing
> And *Zero* at the Bone—

Activities of this type can have two effects. They can give the student an insight into what distinguishes literary language from commonplace language, and they can encourage the student to transfer this insight into his or her own writing. Each year literally *thousands* of students enter college without the sense that a human being is on the other side of the writing exchange, a human being who needs an occasional jolt.

Closure and the Concept of "Out of Context"

Thus far, the argument has been that context is the essential clue in determining word meaning. If this line of reasoning is accepted, it can be further argued that words or phrases taken out of context can be misleading. Recently, the *Texas Monthly* awarded a "bum steer" award (given to Texas public officials who have made the most outrageous statements) to Dallas Police Chief Don Byrd. Byrd was quoted as saying, "If you put two women together in a squad car, they fight. If you put a man and a woman together, they fornicate." He was also quoted as saying, "The niggers have to wear badges to keep them from killing each other." Byrd claimed he was quoted out of context.

While it is doubtful that Mr. Byrd's comments would have looked any better in context, the tendency of newscasters and others to take words and phrases out of context is a process that students should understand. Recall the Jimmy Carter interview in *Playboy*, in which he accused former President Johnson of lying and cheating. The news media seized this quote with feroc-ity; yet the interview as a whole gave a much different impres-sion. Carter glowingly praised Johnson's work for civil rights, and he told of the abuse he suffered for supporting Johnson in 1964. The purpose of this is not to exonerate President Carter—he hardly needs that now—but to suggest that as we come to rely more and more on television for news, we inevitably face the problem of statements being distorted by taking words and phrases out of context. Media obviously cannot quote entire speeches. Reporters must excerpt and the process of distortion, deliberate or not, begins.

This process is not limited to newscasters. Politicians them-selves do it; advertisers do it; and even academic scholars do it. This form of deception is especially insidious because of the seeming truthfulness of quoting the actual words someone spoke. When one sees the word *dazzling* excerpted from a review, it could mean that the entire show was *dazzling* (this would surely be the intent of the advertiser), or the quotation could have been taken from a sentence such as: "Although the costumes were dazzling, the acting, direction, and script were simply terrible." So what does *dazzling* mean? It depends on the context.

Here are two activities which might help sensitize students to the inherent dangers of taking words or phrases out of context: (1) Have students take a book or movie advertisement which quotes a word, phrase, or sentence from a review, and then find the review and determine whether the quotation gives an accurate impres-sion of the review as a whole. (2) Have students locate a moderate to negative review of a movie or book, and by taking words or phrases out of context design an advertisement which distorts the review.

These are only a few possibilities for teaching basic skills using the cloze procedure in the classroom. _____, you can think of others.

References

Rankin, Earl F., and Culhane, Joseph W. "Comparable Cloze and Multiple-choice Comprehension Test Scores." *Journal of Reading* 13: 193-98.

Tomas, D.A. *A Comparative Study of the Contextual Clues Found in Prose and Poetry Forms of Literary Discourse.* Ann Arbor: University Microfilms, Inc., 1977.

Transitions: A Key to Mature Reading and Writing

Evelyn B. Melamed, Hunter College of CUNY
Harvey Minkoff, Hunter College of CUNY

Despite universal agreement that learning to reason is an important part of education, many students can neither follow nor construct a logical argument, since they have not mastered the transitional phrases essential to mature reading and writing. Indeed, many college freshmen would not understand the previous sentence because of its interplay of ideas and transitions.

Examining the larger implications of this inability is too great a digression, but one fact is easy to isolate: while students correctly use connectives such as *but, though,* and *because* in speech, they have considerable difficulty with transitions in reading and writing. In reading, they often cannot comprehend unfamiliar connectives or follow an argument. In writing, they cannot find the connective that is both logically and grammatically required for their purpose. What follows is a series of analytical exercises used in our developmental reading and writing courses that has proved successful in teaching one basic element of written language: transitional phrases.

The meanings of the connectives themselves are a major obstacle to masterful use of transitional phrases. Since normal speech uses only a small number of transitional phrases, the others must be learned as part of one's reading vocabulary. Most textbooks list the connectives and their "definitions," but transitional phrases do not have meanings in the sense of synonyms, the sense that students associate with definitions. Rather, they are structural signals that refer to contextual relationships. Thus, the best way for students to learn the meanings of connectives is for them to first understand the logical relations that connectives signal and then to become familiar with the phrases in context.

One effective classroom technique is to have students analyze pairs of sentences and determine whether their implications are similar, different, sequential, cause and result, or generalization and particular. For example, in the pair

There is no arguing with taste.

Everyone is entitled to his or her own opinion.

both sayings have the same implication: some disagreements cannot be resolved in terms of right and wrong. In contrast, the pair

What is sauce for the goose is sauce for the gander.

One man's meat is another man's poison.

is contradictory: the first sentence implies that if something was good enough for one person it is good enough for another; the second denies this.

Of course, not all relationships are self-evident. The pair

Blessed be the name of the Lord.

The Lord gives and the Lord takes away.

has caused several heated theological confrontations between students who accept the biblical *because* relationship and students who insist on an *even though* interpretation. Such valid differences of opinion emphasize the need for authors to explicitly signal their intended meanings, and this neatly introduces the next exercise.

When students can consistently analyze logical relationships, they then examine pairs with explicit transitional phrases and try to infer the use of the less common, but more sophisticated, connectives. A typical exercise is:

1. What is sauce for the goose is sauce for the gander; *nevertheless*, one man's meat is another man's poison.

2. There is no arguing with taste; *moreover*, everyone is entitled to his or her own opinion.

3. *Insofar as* there is no arguing with taste, that's what makes a horse race.

4. *Despite the fact that* fifty million Frenchmen can't be wrong, one person and the truth make a majority.

5. Strike while the iron is hot; *therefore*, don't put off to tomorrow what can be done today.

During the class discussion, students verbalize their analyses, saying of sentence 1, for example: "If the first part is true, I would not expect the second part to be true also. This relationship is signaled by the word *nevertheless.*"

Choosing proper connectives in writing is especially complicated because the writer needs to satisfy not only logic, but grammatical convention as well. Specifically, students have difficulty with the distinction between subordinating conjunctions and conjunctive adverbs, which signal similar relationships but differ in punctuation and placement. Using the same sentences analyzed in the previous exercise, students are shown that *nevertheless* and *despite the fact that* of sentences 1 and 4, and *insofar as* and *therefore* of sentences 3 and 5, have the same meaning but are used differently. At this point, through these and other examples, students are led to induce that two groups of connectives exist. One, containing such connectives as *therefore, nevertheless,* and *moreover,* always appears in the second clause, moves around within that clause, and requires either a semicolon or period between the clauses. The other, containing such connectives as *because, insofar as,* and *despite the fact that,* may appear in either the first or second clause, always stands first in that clause, and requires a comma between the clauses.

Since, unfortunately, there is no way of predicting which connectives belong to which group, a chart like the following is distributed for reference.

Showing Logical Connection

Group 1 *(conjunctive adverbs)*	Group II *(subordinating conjunctions)*
1. Require semicolon or period.	1. Require comma.
2. Move within their clause.	2. Must begin their clause.
3. Clause stands second.	3. Clause stands first or second.

Contrast

nevertheless, nonetheless, however, still	though, while, despite the fact that, whereas

Cause and Result

therefore, consequently, thus, accordingly, hence	because, since, insofar as, inasmuch as, whereas, in that

Sequence

afterwards, then, earlier, later	after, before, since, when, while, as soon as

Similarity

| likewise, moreover, so too, similarly | just as, in the same way that |

Examples

1. It is easy to despise what you can't have; <u>therefore</u>, the fox said the grapes were sour.
2. It is easy to depise what you can't have; the fox, <u>therefore</u>, said that the grapes were sour.
3. <u>Inasmuch as</u> it is easy to depise what you can't have, the fox said that the grapes were sour.
4. The fox said that the grapes were sour, <u>inasmuch as</u> it is easy to despise what you can't have.

Armed with this reference chart, the class then works on a mastery exercise that requires them to analyze a relationship, determine the presence or absence of grammatical subordination on the basis of punctuation, and choose an appropriate connective, avoiding the old standbys like *because* and *though* if possible. The following mastery exercise is consistently successful and popular:

1. Fools rush in where angels fear to tread. _____ he who hesitates is lost.
2. Pride goes before a fall; _____, a haughty spirit goes before destruction.
3. _____ the mind grows old as well as the body, judges should not hold office for life.
4. _____ man must work from sun to sun, woman's work is never done.
5. Take no thought of tomorrow, _____ sufficient unto the day is the trouble thereof.
6. The early bird catches the worm. _____, it is the early worm that gets caught.
7. It is no shame for a person to live and learn, _____ one is old and wise.
8. Confucius said, "I do not instruct the uninterested; _____ I do not help those who fail to try."
9. He makes me lie down in green pastures. _____ he leads me beside the still waters.
10. _____ the spirit is willing, the flesh is weak.

Obviously, we are dealing with the skill of reasoning, and reasoning cannot be learned by rote. Using the approach outlined in this essay, students master the logic of transitional phrases in a linguistically natural way. First they understand the context; then they learn the vocabulary; next they recognize the structure; and finally they produce mature prose.

College Reading and Study Skills: An Assessment-Prescriptive Model

Alice M. Scales, University of Pittsburgh
Shirley A. Biggs, University of Pittsburgh

Many colleges and universities have begun to offer courses in reading and study skills to students with deficiencies in these areas. An approach designed to enhance the development of reading and study skills for all college and university students is the assessment-prescriptive model. This article will explore the role of the instructor and teaching strategies in the context of this model.

Role of the Instructor

The role of the instructor is crucial to the operation of a college reading program (Scales and Biggs 1976). Instructors' key concerns are: (1) ongoing assessment of students' strengths, needs, and interests; (2) productive learning experiences that include instructor–student, small group, and whole class interaction; (3) appropriate methods, materials, and management strategies which facilitate growth and development of reading and study skills; and (4) evaluation of the effectiveness of the class management system.

In general, college reading/study skills programs do provide for adequate initial assessment of the individual student's needs. Paradoxically, as the student's needs change with exposure to appropriate methods and materials, the initial prescriptions are likely to become ineffective. Perhaps this phenomenon accounts for students' initial enthusiasm and subsequent boredom in some college reading programs.

One way of alleviating boredom is by carefully checking the students' progress after each work session. This check will provide clues for needed change. Students should be urged to communicate regularly with the instructor by writing brief notes describing their feelings about their performance on a particular assignment in their prescription. For example, a student may report, "This was easy; I think I can find main ideas anywhere in a paragraph, now," or "I keep getting the conclusion questions wrong even though I think I have a good reason for choosing my answer." These communications can indicate either a positive change in skill acquisition or some difficulty that signals the need for a conference to clarify approaches to drawing logical conclusions.

Some students prefer to communicate orally about their performance on assignments in their prescription; these students should be met with often in brief sessions to discuss progress or lack of progress in specific skills. A quick visual check of assignment results can indicate difficulty or progress. For example, a pattern of incorrect responses on vocabulary assignments in a particular book may indicate a need to review printed directions, a need to provide more oral practice with the instructor or peers, or a need to take another approach in a different book. Of course, consistent perfect scores may signal a need to move on to more challenging material. Whatever the case, the brief instructor–student interaction is crucial in the process of noting changing needs, preventing loss of interest, and promoting growth in needed reading competencies.

Teaching Strategies

Teaching strategies must always be based on prior assessment. The following description of a college student's attempt to improve his reading will illustrate the working assessment-prescriptive model. The model demonstrates how the instructor (1) assesses the student with appropriate measures, (2) develops a prescription based on the assessment, (3) guides the student through prescribed learning activities, (4) provides an opportunity for record-keeping and review, and (5) continues the assessment-prescriptive process until many weak areas are strengthened to satisfaction.

The first step in the assessment process for this college freshman (known hereafter as Jim) was to analyze his perception of his independent reading activities, habits, and abilities. The analysis revealed the following information about Jim's reading activities. He read approximately three hours per day; two hours were for course requirements. Other reading included *Time*, *Newsweek*,

Reader's Digest, and other nonfiction literature. Concerning Jim's reading habits, he stated that he did not hear words or move his lips and throat muscles while reading. Further, he noted that he did skip some words and phrases and reread others. Even though he had little difficulty in remembering what he had read, Jim questioned the appropriateness of skipping words and phrases and rereading. In reference to his reading abilities, Jim noted that he could summarize, outline, locate main ideas and details, make inferences, answer literal questions, handle unfamiliar vocabulary, and use information gained from the text in a logical manner. Finally, the one problem area Jim identified was his inability to vary his reading rate.

Formal and informal assessment measures were administered to determine the nature of Jim's reading behavior. First, a survey test was used to gather formal data: vocabulary, 14.0; comprehension, 13.8; and rate, 319 wpm. Second, informal instruments (such as the ones in the Appendix) were used to assess vocabulary elements: suffixes, 10 out of 10 correct responses; antonyms, 6 out of 10 correct responses; and synonyms, 9 out of 10 correct responses. Third, an assessment of Jim's note-taking skills showed that he had some skill in identifying significant details but could profit from a coding system to increase note-taking speed. Finally, comprehension categories were informally assessed by having Jim read a minimum of six 175-word selections and respond to questions. Results were: main ideas, no errors; supporting details, no errors; conclusions, repeated errors; context clues, no errors; vocabulary, minimum but a specific pattern of errors; and knowledge of content, repeated errors. This assessment determined that Jim should work on varying his reading rate, developing specific vocabulary elements, learning a coding system for note-taking, and developing his comprehension in identified categories.

The second step was to develop a prescription for Jim. It follows.

Varying Reading Rate

1. Participate in the whole class lecture-discussion on strategies for developing reading flexibility.

2. Complete exercises from *Developing Efficient Reading* (1959), pages 31–37.

3. Complete exercises from *Developing Reading Versatility* (1973), chapter 2, "Scanning Skills"; chapter 3, "Skimming Skills."

4. Do the exercise sheets which have been placed in your folder.

Developing Vocabulary

1. Participate in small group and whole class listening, discussing, and writing of basic college-level vocabulary using *How to Develop a College Level Vocabulary* (1968). Study ten words each class session.

2. Complete vocabulary in context exercises from *Vocabulary in Context: Getting the Precise Meaning* (1975). First, study pages 5–12; next, discuss directions with instructor; then, complete exercises 1–10.

3. Complete vocabulary exercise number one in *Developing Efficient Reading* (1959).

Developing Comprehension

Drawing conclusions:

1. Participate in small group instructor-designed listening comprehension activities.

2. Do exercise in *Drawing a Conclusion* (1974) from the "Comprehension Skills Series." First, study the directions; next, discuss directions with instructor; then, complete exercises 1–3.

Utilizing knowledge of content:

1. Participate in small group or whole class lecture-discussion entitled "Tactics for Reading and Studying in the Social Sciences."

2. In *How to Read the Social Sciences* (1968), do exercises under step 3, "Analyze for Comprehension"; complete chapter 6, then confer with instructor.

The third step was designed to explain the purpose of the prescription to Jim and to guide him through some of the learning activities. For the initial class session it was suggested that Jim complete the first item under each problem area. Subsequently, Jim decided which problem area he wanted to work on during class sessions and for how long. However, the instructor did encourage him to work on several problem areas during each class session, pointing out the importance of working on a number of problem areas simultaneously.

The fourth step in the model afforded Jim the opportunity to review and keep abreast of his progress. In order to do this, a form for Jim's reading and study skills, as well as a form for organizing weekly activities, was provided by the instructor. The form for organizing weekly activities was simply a listing of the hours for each day of the week. The study skills form is pictured in Figure 1.

Date	Skill	Book	Pages	Type of Exercise	Results/Comments
9-15	reading rate	exercise sheet		rate-builder	150 wpm and it had a lot of new words, too. I think I'll try this when I read my sociology assignment tonight.
9-15	vocabulary	*How to Develop a College Level Vocabulary*	8-9	word parts	9/10 correct responses. Words were very easy to figure out once I learned to pick out the important parts.
9-15	comprehension			listening comprehension	Took some notes, not good ...

Fig. 1. Sample of study skills record form.

At the end of each class session, Jim checked his weekly activities form in order to keep abreast of his activities and filled out his study skills form. This form served as Jim's record of his class performance as well as a record of his personal responses to his performance on the exercises. Also, at the beginning of the following class session, the information recorded on the form provided the opportunity for a brief review of Jim's achievements. This information then provided the basis on which the instructor designed activities for the next step in the prescription.

The final step in applying this model was to continue the assessment-prescriptive process until problem areas were sufficiently ameliorated. As areas of weakness were strengthened and needs changed, the prescription changed correspondingly to meet Jim's new needs. For example, once Jim had developed the skill of analyzing words by dividing them into meaningful components, he was urged to practice by comparing the meanings offered by a study of the context with the meanings he generated using word analyis. The prescription thus moved from a word analysis emphasis to one of contextual analysis.

The above discussion has followed the progress of a single student through the assessment-prescriptive procedure. However, the model can be tailored to meet the needs of any student with deficiencies in reading and study skills.

Appendix

Examples of instructor-devised informal measures for analyzing word identification and vocabulary difficulties follow.

Sample: Informal Measure for Word Identification

Directions: Whenever possible, divide the following nonsense words into syllables, mark the short vowels with an "s," mark the long vowels with an "l," and circle the prefixes and suffixes.

treaphilp   hagloid
apipveel   klurpaephlick
mav   ku
diacomstiration   premuncke
zamup   combloigle

Sample: Informal Measure for Vocabulary

Directions:
1. Examine each word.
2. Identify the elements, i.e., prefix, root, suffix, inflections.
3. Write the prefix, root element, suffix, and inflection(s) in the word.
4. Write a meaning for the word.

Inseparable _____

Biology _____

Ungracious _____

Completely _____

Disrespectful _____

Preservice _____

Repress _____

Captions _____

References

Adams, W. Royce. *Developing Reading Versatility*. New York: Holt, Rinehart and Winston, Inc., 1973.

Braam, Leonard S., and Sheldon, William D. *Developing Efficient Reading*. New York: Oxford University Press, 1959.

Brown, Charles M., and Adams, W. Royce. *How to Read the Social Sciences*. Glenview, Ill.: Scott, Foresman & Co., 1968.

Diederich, Paul B., et al. *Vocabulary for College*. New York: Harcourt Brace Jovanovich, Inc., 1967.

Giroux, James A., ed. *Drawing a Conclusion: When Reading*. Providence, R.I.: Jamestown Publishers, 1974.

Giroux, James A., ed. *Understanding Characters: When Reading*. Providence, R.I.: Jamestown Publishers, 1974.

Pauk, Walter. *Vocabulary in Context: Getting the Precise Meaning*. Providence, R.I.: Jamestown Publishers, 1975.

Scales, Alice M., and Biggs, Shirley A. *Reading for Illiterate and Semi-Literate Adults: An Assessment-Prescriptive Instructional Model*. Speech given at the Annual Reading Conference of the St. Thomas Reading Council, 1976. Available in microfiche from ERIC Document Reproduction Service. 17 p. [ED 126 500]

2 About Teaching Writing: Prewriting Practices

The development of writing skills is a multi-step process; attention to development of pre-writing stage skills facilitates subsequent instruction in writing. The nine articles in this chapter stress the importance of the pre-writing stage. They present ways to introduce basic composition skills such as the analysis, summary, evaluation, outlining and documentation of ideas.

Following a Short Narrative through the Composing Process

Walter J. Lamberg, University of Texas at Austin

Basic composing skills can be introduced to students through practice in writing the short, autobiographical narrative. The skills involve learning to use questions to direct one's writing, so that the composition has sufficient focus and expansion. Autobiography was chosen because it seems to be one of the easiest types of writing for students to do. The procedures were developed by me, refined by Daniel Wolter, and tested under experimental conditions in classrooms with secondary and elementary students.[1]

The Assignment. Various versions of the directions were tested to determine the most effective wording. The following version proved to be helpful:

> Write a narrative or story about one interesting incident that happened to you. Choose an incident that happened in less than one day. Include all the important details that answer these questions: What was it about? What happened? Who did it happen to? Who else was involved? Why did it happen? When did it happen? Where did it happen? Try to write as much as you can, at least one page.

The directions were very elaborate because most students seemed to need the expectations for their performance spelled out very specifically. The inclusion of the questions and the suggestion for length were dictated by the finding that most students tended to write a very short, incomplete summary of the incident rather than a complete, detailed account. Though highly structured, the assignment allowed for a wide range of interest, experience, and ability.

---

1. Daniel R. Wolter, "Effect of Feedback on Performance on a Creative Writing Task" (Ph.D. diss., The University of Michigan, 1975); and Walter J. Lamberg, "Design and Validation of Instruction in Question-directed Narrative Writing, Developed Through Discrimination Programming," in ERIC/EDRS: 097 689; abstracted in *Resources in Education* (March, 1975), p. 41.

The Task Analysis. The first step in developing the assignment was to analyze the task of narrative writing. Smith describes task analysis as a process of first identifying the key units of the content to be learned, then identifying the responses students must learn to make to those units of content.[2] The key units for a narrative are the set of seven questions listed in the directions to this assignment. The students' responses are the written answers to each of these questions.

Specifying questions is, of course, an old idea used in journalism; the good news story answers the six interrogatives. The idea is also indebted to instructional procedures in reading. Research in reading has demonstrated that students comprehend and remember better when presented with questions prior to reading or during reading than do students who do not see the questions until after reading.[3] The research supports the practice of giving students "study-guide questions" and of teaching them to ask their own questions before and during their reading.[4] Similarly, students can be taught to direct their writing with questions.

Criteria. Some students were able to write good narratives once the questions were specified; most needed more specific performance criteria. Moffett, in his discussion of narrative writing, identifies two key qualities: focus and expansion.[5] Students must learn to focus their narratives on a key incident, the size of which is appropriate for the length and type of composition. Moffett suggested that the incident be one of less than twenty-four hours duration. (Macrorie has a similar idea of focus.[6]) Having narrowed down their "topic," students then must learn to expand or elaborate their account of the incident through specific detail.

---

2. Donald E. P. Smith, *A Technology of Reading and Writing*, vol. 1, *Learning to Read and Write: A Task Analysis* (New York: Academic Press, 1976), pp. 3-4.

3. Richard C. Anderson and W. Barry Biddle, "On Asking People Questions About What They Are Reading," in *Psychology of Learning and Motivation*, vol. 9, ed. Gordon H. Bower (New York: Academic Press, 1975), pp. 91-93.

4. Francis P. Robinson, "Study Skills for Superior Students in Secondary School," *The Reading Teacher*, 15 (September, 1961): 29-33; Richard Ballard and Walter J. Lamberg, *Teaching the Picture and Text Survey* (Ann Arbor: Office of Instructional Services, the University of Michigan, 1974).

5. James Moffett, *A Student-Centered Language Arts Curriculum, Grades K-6: A Handbook for Teachers* (Boston: Houghton-Mifflin, 1973), pp 213-229.

6. Ken Macrorie, *Writing to be Read* (New York: Hayden, 1968), pp. 5-15; 99-111.

· These two "lessons" are critical. Inexperienced and unsuccessful writers tend to say too little about too much, e.g., *what I did last summer, what happened to me in elementary school.* There are cognitive and affective, as well as skill objectives here. The student learns to understand and appreciate that a piece of good writing tends to say a good deal about a little. Often, the major part of a story (or even the entire story) is an elaboration of an incident that lasted only a few minutes (see Updike's *A&P,* and other stories in J. Moffett's *Points of View*).[7]

Self-provided Feedback. How can the need for good, specific details be explained to students? One way would be to have students write a narrative, then return it with "not enough good specific detail" noted in red ink. An alternative is to have students provide *themselves* with information about their current performance which will affect future performance. Wolter and I experimented with different graphs and charts, such as the "Feedback Chart for Narrative Writing." A student evaluates personal performance in a consistent, objective way, and plots the total points on a progress graph. Each time the student writes, he or she can *see* progress.

Feedback Chart for Narrative Writing

Narrative # _____   Name _____

Read your narrative and figure your points for each question.

	Goal	Your points
1. What Was It About?		
a. One incident	1	_____
b. Less than twenty-four hours	1	_____
c. Happened to you	1	_____
Count each detail that answers	at least	
2. What happened?	10	_____
3. Who did it happen to?	5	_____
4. Who else was involved?	5	_____
5. When did it happen?	5	_____
6. Where did it happen?	5	_____
7. Why did it happen?	5	_____
	Total	_____

---

7. James Moffett and Kenneth R. McElheny, eds., *Points of View: An Anthology of Short Stories* (New York: New American Library, 1966).

Appropriate Models. To learn to use the feedback system, students analyzed sample narratives. In doing that, they were presented with models of good writing *appropriate for them.* For inexperienced writers, the best models may not be literary short stories or narratives written by professional journalists, but good narratives written by their peers, ones similar in language, length, and subject to their own writing. The students read the models critically to see how another writer answered the questions they were going to answer.

A Process-Approach. A few years ago, some of our colleagues got the notion that the reason students wrote poorly was that they had nothing to say. I never met such students. However, I have met students who could *tell* good stories, but much was lost in the translation into writing. What they needed, I think, was a process or series of steps for getting what they could say onto paper. And, having done that, they needed an audience for *what* they said (not just *how* they said it).

Moffett's Memory Writing exercise, which has such a process, was explicitly related to the set of seven questions.[8] First, students addressed "What was it about?" They wrote a list of incidents, finally picking the best subject from a number of possible ones. Next, they addressed "What happened?" by writing a first draft. Then they expanded upon the draft by adding details in answer to the other questions.

Repeated Practice. Students were not limited to one narrative; they practiced by writing several, receiving feedback on each before going on to the next. Giving students only one opportunity to do a type of writing is testing, not teaching. This one-chance approach is terribly common and terribly unfortunate. It denies the majority the opportunity to learn. It results in unproductive, incorrect assumptions about the student's capacity to learn. It leads to unproductive, incorrect assumptions on the student's part about the nature of learning to write and the nature of composing.

The Basics of Composing. Though the immediate concern here is with narrative writing, my ultimate concern was to introduce students to the process of composing. One key "lesson" to be learned was the use of questions to direct the process. I believe any assignment can be translated into a set of questions; several examples are listed below. The last example illustrates the most sophisticated performance: the student must identify his or her own questions to address in an expository or persuasive essay.

---

8. James Moffett, *A Student-Centered Language Arts Curriculum, Grades K-6: A Handbook for Teachers* (Boston: Houghton-Mifflin, 1973), pp. 213-299.

1. Explication of a Poem

What is the theme? How is the theme revealed through the literal situation? (What happened?) The persona? (Who is speaking?) Imagery? Metaphor? Symbol? Form?

2. Discussion of Character

Who is the character? What is his or her role?
What does the author say that tells about him or her?
What does the author show about him or her?
(What does _____ do? Say? What do other characters do or say to _____? What do other characters say about _____?)

3. Essay in Definition

What class does _____ belong to? How does _____ differ from members of its class? What are examples of _____? How does _____ function?

4. Persuasive Essay (Student-Selected Subject and Topic)

How should the school respond to student rights (topic)?
What rights should students have? Why?
How are they not respected?
How should they be respected? Why?

The second "lesson" involves the criteria of focus and expansion. In examining essays and research papers written by secondary and college students, I concluded that the same qualities were neglected in those types of writing. Commonly, students tried to write about a whole subject, instead of achieving a focus narrow enough to be handled effectively in the length of the paper. Even when the topic was clear early in the paper, it was often not adequately expanded upon. Key questions were either not addressed in sufficient detail or were neglected altogether.[9] And, typically, students had no means of evaluating themselves as they were going through the process. A set of questions serves as a guide, not only in writing a first draft but also in rewriting. The student asks him/herself: Have I answered my questions? No? Then I need to write more. Have I answered other questions I did not plan to address? Yes? Are they relevant? Should I cut them? Or, go back and rewrite my introduction so that the reader will be prepared for them?

9. For a discussion of problems in academic writing, see Walter J. Lamberg, "Major Problems in Doing Academic Writing," *College Composition and Communication* 28 (1977): pp. 26-29.

The basics of our own school days—the superficialities which become important when you want to make yourself understood—may have been neglected in recent years, but it is the fundamental basics, the basics at the level of "deep structure," that were neglected before. I mean: selecting a topic that was appropriate because (1) it's important to you, (2) you wish to share it with others, and (3) you are able to say enough about it; including details so that the incident is shown, not just told; learning that different types of writing differ in the key questions they answer; learning the differences and similarities between speaking stories and writing them and between writing them and reading them; and, finally, learning that what you had to say and write could be, at times, as alike and unlike, as interesting and uninteresting, and as important and unimportant as anything anyone else could say or write. Forward to those basics.

Teaching Composition through Outlining

Karla F. C. Holloway, Michigan State University

In the academic program of the beginning college student one thing is certain: Freshman Composition. This course is a major challenge to students and teachers alike. The student must endure a barrage of themes and assignments with classmates whose academic interests and abilities run the gamut to be found in the college or university. The teacher must sustain the interest and performance of students who feel they have been funneled into a class simply to fulfill the university requirement of English 101.

None of us in the profession doubts that English 101 is essential for the increasing numbers of college freshmen who enter the university with serious gaps in their language skills. What is disturbing is that these gaps are not only found in such areas as creative writing or advanced literature, but in the most basic of the communication skills, reading and expository writing.

One of the most successful methods I have used in teaching English 101 is reintroducing the student to the value of outlining. I find that teaching the use of the outline, beginning with a basic lesson taught to most students in elementary school, adds significantly to the success of the course. One of my first questions to a class of not-so-eager English 101 students is "Who remembers the five Ws and one H?" I get prompt responses from all sides of the classroom—"Who!" "What!" "When!" "Why!" "How!"—followed by smug smiles ("Aha! I knew the answer to the first question this prof asked!"), then quizzical looks ("Why would she want to call up those old ghosts?"). Satisfied that I have have sparked their curiosity and interest, I explain some "facts" of higher education: (1) The students in this classroom may represent as many as ten different departments in the institution. (2) Each student will be forced to analyze quickly and accurately a wide variety of reference and textual material in the next four years. (3) Students in both this and other classrooms will be expected to express themselves in clear and concise writing. These "facts"

36

represent potential problems for both student and teacher. But I have found that reliance on the outline (directed by the five Ws and one H) as a formal prelude to writing the final draft, is a remarkable solution to the problems. I will address each of the three "facts" with specific reference to the outline as a solution.

Variety of Needs

Although each student has different needs, the fact that practicality demands a collective endeavor is a compelling reason to turn to the outline. This form of skill training adapts as easily to the accounting major as to the zoology major. After learning the students' interests and program plans from their "Who Am I" file cards, I discuss with each of them the requirements of their particular major, using the five Ws and one H. I ask questions such as:

> *Who* would be interested in this program?
>
> *What* does it require?
>
> *When* did the student's interest develop?
>
> *Where* can the student put his or her skills to work?
>
> *Why* did the student choose this program?
>
> *How* can the student explore the extent of his or her interest in the program?

In this way, the first days of Freshman Composition establish for that subject an important relationship with the student's academic goals. And because each student must give individual attention to this collective task, the classroom begins to become a writing laboratory in a very real sense.

In addition, the students begin to develop an ability which will serve them well in future Freshman Composition writing projects, for outlining is a valuable skill whether used for writing argumentation or description. I found that if required far enough in advance of the due date for the finished product, the outline helped students in discussing, during weekly teacher-student conferences, plans for and problems with the assignment. This resolved some difficulties before the revision phase of the writing process began.

Skill of Analysis

Comprehension of a great amount of textual material is often necessary for the composition student preparing to write. Using the outline is a good way to improve reading comprehension. Sample stories from a variety of texts, including a rhetoric selected for classroom use, provide the raw material for sharpening this skill. Carefully planned questions guide the student to abstract the main idea, its subsidiary ideas, and the development and conclusion of those ideas from a selected text. Outlining these stories in a standard form (for example, the method suggested in *Harbrace College Handbook*, 7th edition) gives the student an overview of the subject. I encourage my students to bring to class texts from other subjects, to use the same plan for sections or chapters from those texts, and to study the resulting abstracts. Many students feel that a new way to study has been made available to them and they are glad to adopt outlining as a reliable study method.

When students outline a piece of professional writing, they learn the four necessary elements for their own themes. I have taught these relatively simple, but for most student writers, elusive ideas using musical terminology. The sonata allegro form (SAF) in musical composition comprises an *introduction* to the theme, the *development* of that theme, a *recapitulation* of the original theme, and a *coda* or *conclusion*. In outlines which students have abstracted from given readings, these elements are usually apparent. Of course, it is necessary for the instructor to guide the students to selections which will best exhibit the desired end. At this point, students understand more clearly what is expected of them in the outline and in the finished product. The four elements must also be apparent in the student's own written theme.

Clarity and Direction

Muddled prose is a common characteristic of student writing. What students actually write seldom emerges as clearly on paper as it resided, or as they thought it resided, in their minds. Style, vocabulary, and structure can be problems for the writer. Obviously an outline cannot solve all these problems, but it can pinpoint problem areas. After students have "written out" everything on their minds pertaining to the subject, giving little attention to form and every effort to getting a lot said, I often ask them to try to "talk through" each part of the outline. In this way students have an opportunity to organize their thoughts orally, one of the surest methods of helping them discover for themselves where the problem lies. For some reason, hearing oneself stumble through a muddled thought makes the problem as well as the solution easier to approach.

The controlling form of an outline encourages clarity in the theme. When students see their ideas organized in outline form, they are almost forced to select carefully and organize effectively the ideas from their rough draft as they begin to write their final theme. The concepts of introduction, development, recapitulation, and conclusion are also easy to illustrate within the outline's controlling framework.

The W and H questions introducing the methodology of an outline serve as additional reassurance for skeptical students. Because they are often afraid they haven't enough to say or have said everything they can think of, I remind them to keep this list handy. Answering these questions in an assignment often expands a poorly developed idea into a complete and informative discussion. Fortunately, the ample prewriting notes and freely written drafts supply raw material for students who would otherwise have "nothing to say."

Returning to the very basic principle of writing from an outline may seem to be a simplistic solution to the many problems encountered by student and teacher in English 101. Rather than being a final solution to all these problems, the outline and six questions lead the student to identify in an organized fashion some of the problems of form and style in composition. In addition to functioning as a dependable tool for the student who has always viewed composition with trepidation, the method replaces haphazard forays into composition with solid and thoughtful approaches at the logical point in the writing process.

A Workable Approach to Teaching Composition

Susan Belasco Smith, McLennan Community College, Waco, Texas

A year or two ago, I observed on an English teacher's bulletin board a poster entitled "How to Write a Composition." Hoping for some helpful instructions to use in my own classroom, I read the chart carefully, and was dismayed to read the following rules.

1. Use ink and leave margins on either side of the page.
2. Begin each sentence with a capital letter and end each sentence with a period.
3. Spell each word correctly.
4. Indent each paragraph.
5. Do not use "and" to connect sentences.

These superficial guidelines are indicative of the problem faced by the composition teacher at any grade level. We know what a composition should look like, but we are often unprepared and ill-equipped to teach our students how to construct the paragraphs they are supposed to indent. Teaching composition, for most of us, is perplexing because our teacher education has provided us with little guidance in this area. While most of us can prepare sound lessons on the characteristics of an epic, few of us feel on such firm ground when the time comes for a lesson in composition. The very thought of grading seventy-five to one hundred papers is enough to overwhelm even the most enthusiastic first-year teacher. Perhaps because my initial teaching experience was in teaching composition as a graduate teaching assistant, I was forced to develop some methods for teaching composition that I believe can make writing more stimulating and even enjoyable for both teachers and students. First, I had to decide that teaching composition is far more than coercing reluctant students to write papers on characterization, setting, point of view, structure, theme, or symbolization in novels. Composition should be an experience in which students learn to organize their thoughts, think through a problem, employ realistic detail, and express themselves in understandable, coherent language. A simple but workable method for beginning a composition unit can accomplish this.

At the beginning of the course, I introduce composition with an assignment involving the preparation and execution of a paragraph relating some process. Everyone has some experience in giving directions or instructions or in showing others how to perform some task, and I build my lesson around this experience. I begin by asking volunteers to explain how to do something. Typically, response is slow at first, but, with encouragement, the students soon become involved in telling the class how to make a terrarium, bake a cake, change a tire, start a car, make a friend, drive a tractor, waste time, and even, as on one occasion, how to annoy a teacher. Then I explain to the students that they have already mastered the first essential step in writing: choosing an idea and thinking it through. At this point, no student can protest that he or she has nothing to write about. The commitment to a topic has been made before the class.

From this discussion I move to an explanation of organizing information. I ask each student to write his or her topic choice, the process he or she described earlier, at the top of a sheet of paper, which I call the planning paper. Then each student lists the steps involved in his or her particular process. After giving the students some time to work this out, I walk around the room, checking the lists. Many students tend to make lengthy lists of detailed steps. For example, if the process is about baking a cake, the student might list all the ingredients (flour, sugar, eggs, and shortening) as well as all the necessary utensils (bowls, measuring cups, mixer, and pans). At this point, I feel that it is important to explain to the students that the major steps in a process must be emphasized by grouping parts of the process into specific areas. Returning to the example of baking a cake, I might suggest that all of the small steps involving the ingredients and utensils be grouped under the general heading of "assembling ingredients and utensils." The details can be used to explain this heading within the body of the paragraph. Each student should proceed until he or she has two or three major steps with supporting details listed for each separate one.

The students are now ready to write their topic sentences. In an effort to promote clear, organized thinking, I ask the students to

Basics in Composition: Fluency First

R. Baird Shuman, University of Illinois at Urbana-Champaign

A universal complaint among composition students at nearly every level is that they have nothing to write about, that they just cannot get started, that they are intimidated by the prospect of trying to fill a blank page. The conversion of thoughts to words, phrases, and sentences strikes terror in the hearts of even some professional writers, so it is not difficult to sympathize with students who feel the same sort of terror when they are called upon to engage in that highly creative exercise known as composing. From nothing they must make something; from point zero they must achieve 500 or 700 or 1,000 words.

In order to help my students overcome their difficulty, I ask them early on to make something from another something which I provide. I ask that, rather than starting at point zero, they begin at point five or seven or ten. Also, I do not require a specific number of words, but rather suggest continuous writing for a given length of time, ranging from three to fifteen or twenty minutes, depending on the type of approach I am using.

Specifically, I attempt to use initial writing exercises, such as the two that follow, to provide impetus for writing and to establish in the minds of students the confidence that they can indeed write in considerable quantity. While I am working to help students achieve fluency, I pay little attention to mechanical correctness, standard usage, and other such matters. I consider them of great importance, but I am wholly convinced that in the natural order of things fluency must come before correctness.

I find that dozens of means can be used to help students achieve fluency. The two which I am about to describe have worked extremely well with youngsters who have come into classes and workshops that I have conducted asking for more writing assignments like these two.

The first exercise is a simple one. Make sure that each student and that you, the teacher, have blank sheets of paper and pens or pencils. Say to the class, "When I say 'Go,' begin writing about anything you like. If you have nothing to write about, just write over and over again a word like *phantom* or *calliope* or *mosquito*—any word that strikes your fancy. But, and this is very important, *no matter what, do not stop writing until the timer goes off.* Go." I usually set the timer for three minutes and we all write furiously. When the bell sounds, we stop even if we are in the middle of a word. I then collect the papers, redistribute them, and say, "Read what you have on the paper you have just received. Take up where the first writer left off. Write until the bell sounds. Go."

I usually allow three or four exchanges, asking at the end of the final exchange that the students take a minute after the bell sounds to finish the paper. Then we read some of the papers aloud, which is a very popular activity. It is not unusual for both sides of the paper to be full from top to bottom and margin to margin, indicating that fluency has been achieved. Also, the student who begins with 75 or 100 repetitions of a single word eventually begins writing, if not before the first exchange, surely before the second. And a student who receives a paper on which *phantom* or *mosquito* has been written 75 or 100 times has never in my experience continued the repetition.

Another fluency exercise that I use with particular success when I work with students who are disabled in both reading and writing is what I call the "Even-Steven Swap Game." I give students ten words and ask them, working singly, in pairs, or in larger groups, to swap me a story for the ten words. The story must use each word at least once. My words are the ten most difficult or the ten longest words in a news story, usually a rather sensational one. A typical list includes *deliberations, homicide, investigation, manslaughter, negligent, perpetually, supermarket, testimony, 38-caliber,* and *verdict.* Any story generated from this combination of words would probably involve a crime and subsequent trial. The students' imaginations provide the details, and they do so rather easily because they are working from point ten, not point zero.

When the papers have been completed, I usually distribute the story from which I took my list of words, so that students can compare their outcomes with the source from which their words came. This exercise encourages fluency by providing a minimal context. It also encourages dictionary work because students do not always know the words they are given. When students work in groups, usually all but one or two of the words can be defined by someone in the group, and this is to the good. I also provide definitions when I feel it is appropriate to do so, particularly with students who recognize only three or four of the words. Sometimes all I have to do is pronounce the word and a student recognizes it.

The written work that results from these exercises usually is peppered with errors in mechanics and usage, but quantitatively it is impressive. Also, the students' writing usually provides a nucleus from which to work first on proofreading—"Go through and catch all the spelling errors you can; change anything you don't like or that sounds wrong to you; make sure your punctuation is the way you want it"—and then on revision.

I prefer that proofreading and revision exercises be group activities because, no matter how many deficiencies the individual students in a class might have in written expression, they all have some strengths as well. The collective grammatical knowledge of any five people is quite impressive even though each of the five may be receiving Ds and Fs in English. Students learn much more from engaging in proofreading and revision collectively than they do from having a teacher red-pencil their papers. Also, they can accept criticism much better in a nonthreatening group situation than some of them can from an authority figure like a teacher. Students who are engaged in task-oriented activities learn more and, in the long run, are much less disruptive than students who are lectured to by a teacher from the front of the classroom.

Once the proofreading has been done and mechanical imperfections corrected, students should be encouraged to do the sort of real revision which is often neglected. This is the revision that requires students to experiment with new ways of saying things. They might be made aware of such matters as sentence variety: "Do you have mostly short sentences or long sentences? Can you combine (or divide) some of your sentences? What happens when you do this? Which version do you prefer?" They might try to aim their writing at a specific audience: "Can you rewrite this as a newspaper report? As a police report? As a letter from the victim to someone he/she loves?"

Nothing is more basic to effective writing than revision. Revision should be preceded and followed by proofreading to catch careless errors, but proofreading should not be confused with revision. The two processes, while complementary, are not identical. Also basic to effective writing is the ability to achieve fluency, for the physical task of putting ideas on paper must precede both proofreading and revision. Students who concentrate too much on correctness while they are involved in the process of translating their ideas into words will not achieve fluency unless they have an unusually good command of the mechanics of expression, and many students have not yet achieved this command. Therefore, teachers will achieve the best results in writing classes if they work on fluency first and then, through group activity, on proofreading and revision.

The Great American One-Sentence Summary

Silver Stanfill, Anchorage Community College of the University of Alaska

Summarizing is a basic skill needed in many academic and job situations, a skill to be presented and practiced at just about every educational level, from early childhood language development activities ("What did Marcus say about his picture?") to graduate school ("What's the most important word in Jonathan Swift's *Examiner* essay of November 23, 1710?" [The answer is *ingratitude*.]).

When students can survey material to determine its purpose, main idea(s), and major divisions, they're ready for lessons and practice in summarizing. With my community college students, I've had some good results and super side effects from a simple formula for a one-sentence summary:

1. Identify the thing being summarized;
2. tell what it *begins with*;
3. tell what's in the middle (or what it's mostly about; helpful with wording are *covers*, *discusses*, *presents*, and *develops the idea that . . .*);
4. tell what it *ends with*.

I begin with the formula written on the board (or overhead), and work with groups to fill in the wording for each part of the formula. Then we add the connections to turn the list of details into a sentence. To smooth out the sentence, sometimes it helps to reorder the details. When the students begin using the formula on their own, they understand that merely listing the four parts in a column on their papers provides them with the meat of their summary sentences.

It's best to start using the formula with materials already familiar to the students—chronologically-ordered narratives like fairy tales (not news stories!) are ideal. After in-class practice on "Goldilocks," "Little Red Riding Hood," and "Snow White," my composition students went on to out-of-class one-sentence summaries of autobiographies like *The Diary of Anne Frank* and *Nigger*.

Logically-ordered exercises would come next. Try the formula in summarizing a text chapter; then try summarizing the summary of a text chapter. Later work with materials demanding the use of critical reading skills: first, in judging the relative emphasis an author gives various subtopics; next, in establishing a *personal* idea of the relative importance of subtopics; and still later, in recognizing and explaining the significance of repeated images or related imagery. Students successful at these levels are ready for précis-writing. (For students with college-level skills, I recommend Lincoln's "Gettysburg Address" for the three kinds of critical reading/summarizing practice suggested here.)

When students are comfortable with the formula and its demands, I begin in-class exercises with a time limit. Here's where the super side effects come in.

In my Study Skills micro-courses I set aside the last five minutes of each session for students to write a one-sentence summary of that day's class on a 3 x 5 card. On their way out of class, they drop the cards in an envelope by the door.*

Usually it takes me less than half an hour to go through a set of cards—taking attendance from them as I go. I mark and make comments (I insist that the back be left free for my use) or just put a check on each card to indicate I have no particular comments. In each set I mark at least one (and sometimes several) with a star that means "Please write this on the board right away." I try never to embarrass a student, so good or best examples are the ones starred (and if necessary, marked with corrected spelling). As students enter the classroom, they pick up their cards from last time, and the starred ones are written on the board as class begins.

We spend the first few minutes of class on those sentences—helpful for returning absentees. Early in the course I choose sentences to help the class understand accuracy in summarizing:

Is this what the class WAS about?

---

*A note about the advantages of 3 x 5 cards: stiff stock and small size. Limiting students to one side helps both to allay fears of not having enough to say and to forestall verbosity; and a set of cards is easier to handle than a pile of papers.

Is anything important left out?

Are these details in the right order?

Are they an accurate reflection of relative emphasis?

Later we work with sentence structure and style:

How easy is this to read?

How can we change it to read more smoothly?

Any ineffective repetitions? Any needless words?

I ask the students to compare their sentences with the ones on the board, and, if they like, to revise and resubmit their cards. Since the course is pass/withdraw, neither dismal attempts nor plagiarized revisions affect a student's grade; but students *do* revise! They say they like the one-sentence summary formula; they say it helps them in thinking, reading, and writing.

I think the formula works—if used on materials students are ready for. Moreover, a set of summaries of the class I've just taught is invaluable immediate feedback. I find out right away who's missing main points, and who's having a hard time saying what he or she thinks. Most important, I learn how my perception of what-went-on-in-there differs from the class's.

The summaries are especially useful for sessions involving guest speakers. Knowing what's coming up at the end of the hour, speakers are a little more careful about preparation and a little less apt to digress; students have a chance to practice being more alert and/or tactful than usual, and I get a chance to practice— from scratch—the formula that I preach. After a guest speaker, I usually find in each set of cards at least one student summary that's better than mine, entirely or partly. This is one basic skill strategy that's got something for everybody.

> Beginning with a brief explanation of the significance of summary-writing skill, "The Great American One-Sentence Summary" presents a 4-part formula for developing that skill, discusses methods and benefits of using the formula, and ends with a summary of the article itself.

Human Values in Farmer McGregor's Garden

June B. Evans, L.W. Higgins High School, Marrero, Louisiana

The Tale of Peter Rabbit in a plain brown wrapper? Such was the initial response by an eleventh-grade honors section to a recent research assignment in English literature.

Did they dare sandwich *The Wind in the Willows* between copies of *Chemistry* and *Advanced Mathematics*?

Could they keep straight faces as they signed charge slips for *Charlotte's Web* and *Johnny Crow's Garden*?

Happily, by the end of the two and one-half week unit scheduled between Christmas vacation and mid-year examinations, they had, indeed, dared. And the results were rewarding: they now viewed "kiddie lit" as functional literature for children in its revelation of cultural/social mores, interpersonal relationships, ideals, and models to pattern after.

As part of a sequence in skills-building for writing research papers, this is a unit which would appear, at first glance, to be relatively simple; at this point the students are already writing five-paragraph essays with outlines, footnotes, and bibliography. The next objective is to illustrate to them how different papers can be produced while utilizing identical source material. This requires an original search through primary sources, followed by a synthesis of the accumulated data.

The unit is based on the use of anthropomorphism of animals in children's literature. Groups of five or six students work collectively on researching and discussing the organization of an assigned topic; each student then writes a documented essay based on the reading and research.

Prefaced by Samuel Johnson's comment that "what is written without effort is in general read without pleasure," the seven blocks of information about the assignment are arranged randomly on a duplicated sheet and distributed to each student at the end of a class period. Students are instructed to locate copies of the books listed, since the project is scheduled to begin the next day. Usually, a twenty-four-hour delay before a discussion of project directions results in fewer distracting comments and will elicit more constructive and perceptive questions about procedure and objectives.

To foster a relaxed informality in this discussion, the information on the sheet does not adhere to the conventions of outlining, but is presented as seven unnumbered boxes of data connected by eye-directing arrows.

Box A.
Literary Terms to Review:
    tone
    imagery
    structure
    point of view
    satire

Box B.
Subject Headings for Parallel Reading in Psychology and Sociology:
    anthropomorphism
    learning
    self-discovery
    personality
    behavior
    motivation
    individual differences
    emotion

Box C.
Elements:
    title page
    outline
    essay
    footnotes
    bibliography
    end sheet

Box. D.
Time Table (Day 1–Day 13):
    –time to read (individually)
    –time to research (individually)
    –time to discuss (with group)
    –time to write (individually)

Box E. Read as Many as Possible:

The Wind in the Willows (K. Grahame)
Animal Farm (G. Orwell)
Tale of Peter Rabbit (B. Potter)
Charlotte's Web (E.B. White)
The Story of Dr. Dolittle (H. Lofting)
Alice's Adventures in Wonderland (L. Carroll)
Through the Looking Glass (L. Carroll)
Johnny Crow's Garden (L. Brooke)
Rabbit Hill (R. Lawson)

Box F. Discuss Your Group's Assigned Topic:

1. Anthropomorphism of Animals in Children's Reading as a Revelation of Interpersonal Relationships
2. Anthropomorphism of Animals in Children's Reading as a Revelation of Ideals and Models to Pattern After
3. Anthropomorphism of Animals in Children's Reading as a Revelation of Cultural/Social Mores, Conventions, and Institutions
4. Anthropomorphism of Animals in Children's Reading: Satirical, Realistic, Sentimental
5. Anthropomorphism of Animals in Children's Reading: A Chronologic Progression to More Realistic and Objective Treatment

Box G. Sample Form for Weekly Log Kept Daily and Turned in Each Friday:

Date	Subjects or Titles Read	No. of Pages	Hours

The list of authors' works constitutes the minimum number of selections to be read; however, the more enterprising students do search for similar books by other authors and for parallel reading in psychology and sociology.

A high-school library most probably will not include all of the specified titles in its collection, but that is no deterrent to a class of industrious and competitive students. By going to different branches of the public library and to neighbors and friends, they soon locate multiple copies of each title, and the project commences—with much light-hearted banter about the reading level of their assigned material.

One week and six or seven books later, the banter will have changed to serious consideration of what their younger brothers and sisters are (or are not) gaining by reading such literary classics. Students puzzle over the authors' use of complex sentences, the polysyllabic word choices, the subtle nuances of illustrations; they see real people—people they recognize—in Toad of Toad Hall, in Wilbur, in Peter Rabbit's mother; and they identify with Alice's attempts at self-discovery. Once they begin to sense this serious realm of ideas and ideals, their problem becomes what to do with the material. This is where the group process is extremely effective with students who are capable of discussing and organizing objectively without feeling threatened by peer criticism.

Having settled on a tentative outline for the treatment of the group's assigned topic, each student begins accumulating data on the perennial 3 x 5 cards, source number at upper right, page reference at lower right, and working outline section at upper left. (I suggest use of a penciled notation for the outline designations to facilitate future rearrangement of items.)

Each class period now is used as the group prefers. Since the students are working against a specific end-of-semester deadline, they determine their priorities for the reading, compiling notes, discussing, and writing. Thus, instead of my discussing individual plans of organization with each of twenty-eight students, minor problems are resolved within each of the five discussion groups. I am consulted as final arbitrator of the occasional impasse.

The practicality of note-taking on 3 x 5 cards rather than on standard-size notebook paper is now reluctantly accepted as useful and necessary instead of cumbersome, as they decide (some groups more than once) to rearrange their components in a more workable order.

At two five-day intervals, each student submits a daily log of time spent in reading; admittedly, this is merely a device to discourage procrastination. Since the last week involves the actual writing, no other reading log is required.

Most of the students begin their rough drafts, after a final group discussion about statement of thesis and structure of outline, within five days of the due date. The final draft is handwritten, double-spaced, on unlined paper, with footnotes positioned in the lower portion of each appropriate page. Some critical writing problems surface when a final version is evolving from a rough draft. Allowing students class time for some of this final writing gives an opportunity for immediate teacher conferences. Questions on the myriad details inherent in this type of writing are obviously much more likely when you are readily available. After all, a pride in accuracy is often encouraged by access to information.

The resulting papers, well-organized, easy to evaluate, remarkably perceptive, yet with individual interpretations even within each group, will have remained in the students' own control from start to finish. And, consequently, the students will have supported each other in their insecurity on beginning the project, shared in their frustrations of organization, and solved problems held in common. Thus, the demands placed on each student by the dynamics of the group process serve as impetus to achievement.

Paradoxically, the class writing project becomes in itself a significantly real example of that productive cooperation depicted by the anthropomorphic creatures in the literature for children. The students move forward in acquisition of research skills. And *Peter Rabbit* emerges from that plain brown wrapper as a purveyor of human values.

Investigative Reporting in the Journalism Class

Richard G. Hause, Kansas State University

Many secondary school students enroll in journalism because it's a good elective; it's a break from the routine of the normal English class; it's a chance to do a different type of writing; it's a chance to get out of the classroom and off the campus; it's a possible career choice. The effective journalism teacher can plan activities to fill all of these student expectations. The journalism classroom can be a beehive of meaningful activities every day, not just the day before the paper goes to press.

The utmost concern is, of course, putting out the school newspaper on a regular basis or putting together the school yearbook for distribution sometime during the year. The effective journalism teacher will want to acquaint the students with the fascinating heritage of the newspaper in America and its roots in the growth of the mass media. In order to cover this important aspect and to make journalism fun, flexible, and functional, try the following suggestions.

Begin a unit on investigative writing. The study of this skill affords high school journalism students the opportunity to read, study, analyze, and evaluate resource materials on the history, distant and recent, of the newspaper industry. It is an opportunity to learn about the newspaper while they are using one of the most productive skills in the field of journalism.

Arrange the room to resemble a press room, if possible. Divide students into pairs (a la Bernstein and Woodward of *The Washington Post*). Assign each pair the job of investigating one of the important segments of journalistic history. One pair will investigate the lives of famous personages like Bonfils and Tammen of *The Denver Post* (two fascinating books have been written about their era: *Thunder in the Rockies* by Bill Hosokawa and *Timberline* by Gene Fowler), William Allen White and his work with *The*

Emporia Gazette, and William Randolph Hearst and his journalistic empire.

Another pair will study some of the better newspapers (*The New York Times, The Washington Post, The Miami Herald, St. Louis Post-Dispatch,* and *The Christian Science Monitor*) to discover their histories and determine why they are fine newspapers. Don't forget excellent smaller newspapers, perhaps from the local area.

An investigation by one pair into outstanding photojournalists such as Margaret Bourke-White, Alfred Eisenstadt, and Gordon Parks will reveal various contributions to the field and give the students a sense of that heritage. A study of famous columnists such as Erma Bombeck, Ernie Pyle, Ann Landers, Hal Boyle, James Reston, Art Buchwald, and William F. Buckley will help another pair of students gain respect for the daily demands placed on these writers and the impact their writings have made on the newspaper industry. Famous cartoonists such as Chic Young, Al Capp, Mort Walker and Dik Browne, Charles Schultz, Milton Caniff, and more recently Gary Trudeau offer a wide variety of journalistic talents for students' investigations. (Some of these persons might respond to a personal letter or person-to-person telephone call from an enterprising student!) The study of these contributors will add to the fun and perhaps encourage a budding cartoonist. By the same token but in a slightly different vein, the political cartoonists such as Bill Mauldin, Thomas Nast, Walt Kelly, Oliphant, and Herblock will afford two other students a fine taste of political satire and its importance to the media. (Copies of some of their drawings can be obtained by writing directly to the syndicate for whom the cartoonist works.)

Investigation into the filming of newspaper-oriented movies such as *Citizen Kane, Front Page* (both versions for comparison), and *All the President's Men* as well as television shows such as the late *Mary Tyler Moore Show* and an older one entitled *The Doris Day Show* will offer another view of the field.

The basics of journalism will be reviewed through student investigation of the methods used to distribute newspapers worldwide and the emergence of the teletype and other rapid forms of communication. A closer look at the role of the newspaper during war time will give further evidence of its growing importance in society.

The freedom of the press in the past and today as seen in connection with famous trials such as the Charles Manson case, the Watergate case, the case of Daniel Ellsberg, and more recently Daniel Schorr will give one team of students a timely look at newspersons and their responsibilities to their papers and to the public.

Two of the students will surely be interested in the competition that exists between newspapers in getting the story first, getting the big story, taking the rare or only photograph, or solving crimes against the state. An investigation will reveal several historic examples of the stiff competition that has existed in the past and continues today.

During the investigation period, the teacher will act as the editor-in-chief, offering suggestions for resource materials, persons to consult, and investigative techniques used to uncover evidence. Draw the class or staff together every other day to hold a briefing on what important leads are being uncovered, what areas still remain a mystery, what resources can be shared, and how to progress from that point. Stress the importance of holding one's judgment until all the facts are in and evaluated for accuracy.

The closing session of the unit will resemble a staff meeting in a newspaper office. The editor will call on each investigating team to present an oral summary of its findings. The staff will critique each group's findings in light of their accuracy, objectivity, significance in journalistic history, educational value, and reader appeal. The staff will then decide which groups will be encouraged to revise their findings and present them as a feature article in the school newspaper some time during the school year.

When the articles are published, the journalistic investigators will have experienced a full cycle of investigative news reporting from conception to fruition. The students will surely come away from this experience with a greater appreciation of journalism and its roots. They will have shared their work with students outside the journalism class, and these students may, in turn, become better informed consumers of the media.

The Research Paper: Getting Started

Alma S. Freeman, Alabama State University

Teaching conventional research techniques is a standard requirement in many freshman English courses. Traditionally, two approaches have been used: the "free" approach, which allows a student to select and limit a topic, read about it in books and periodicals, take notes, and write a long, documented paper; or the "controlled" approach, which requires each student to use materials pre-assembled in a text and permits an entire class to work within the same field of subject matter—selecting and limiting a topic within the prescribed field, reading essays from the text, taking notes, and writing and documenting the final paper. With both approaches, the instructor usually hands the students preconceived topics for research and then structures the class sessions around the steps in one of the many research paper manuals currently on the market. Little, if anything, is done to tap the students' own interests, experiences, and ideas.

Innovative English teachers, seeking to teach the basic skills more effectively, want more interesting and challenging ways of teaching the research paper, and especially for initiating research projects. Because I believe that teaching/learning begins with the students, with their own interests and experiences, I suggest a sequence of student-centered activities that may aid teachers and students in getting started with the research paper. These activities are designed to establish an appropriate climate and spirit for research, to motivate students and get them involved in their own learning, and to assist students in exploring their own resources before they begin to research those of other people.

Peter Elbow, author of *Writing Without Teachers* (London: Oxford University Press, 1973), poses an interesting and, I think, workable theory for handling writing activities. The writing process, Elbow believes, consists of two parts: producing and composing. He also believes that teachers must tell students exactly what is required of them, and construct activities to help them achieve that goal. I have adopted Elbow's theories in providing a format for the following outline of activities. Emphasis here is on *producing*.

Preliminary Discussion

Purpose: To tell students exactly what is required for the finished product.

1. Engage the class in a discussion of the nature of research and of the research paper.
2. Summarize the traditional steps in writing the research paper.
3. Provide a sample of what the finished product should look like.
4. Explain that the activities which follow will aid the students in carrying out the steps necessary for writing the final paper.

Filmstrips and/or transparencies are especially suitable for 1, 2, and 3.

Producing

Purpose: To generate subjects and ideas and to define a direction for research.

Finding Subjects of Interest

1. General subjects may evolve from the students through a freewriting exercise.
2. General subjects may evolve from the students through a brainstorming session.
3. The instructor may provide a list of general subjects and, through discussion, have students expand the list.

Selecting and Limiting the Subject/Discovering Direction

1. Freewriting Exercise
   a. Goals of Freewriting
      To relax inhibitions and initiate thought
      To find a subject and a direction for research

To aid the students in getting at their own experience with the subject

b. Guides for Freewriting

After a brief review of the subjects, each student selects one and writes freely about it for approximately 15 to 20 minutes. The students are instructed to write as fast as they can without stopping to ponder a thought, without concern for spelling, grammar, punctuation, or sentence structure. The important thing is to keep the pen moving and get ideas down on the page. They are to write whatever comes to mind about the subject. If nothing comes, they are instructed to write "Nothing comes to my mind" or "I can't think of anything to write" until the thoughts begin to flow. The only requirement is that they *never* stop writing.

2. Brainstorming Session

Following the freewriting activity, the students divide into groups of three to read and discuss each others' freewriting.

a. Goals of the Brainstorming Session

To further relax inhibitions and generate ideas
To identify and state specific topics suitable for research
To formulate research questions for the topic
To identify and state clearly key thoughts about the topic
To identify and state clearly ideas which support and clarify key thoughts
To identify resources to survey

b. Guides for the Brainstorming Session

Each student reads his or her freewriting aloud to the group. Group members may ask such questions as the following about each piece:

What specific aspect of the subject does the piece address? (limits the subjects)
What words and passages seem strongest and most important?
Do they hint at general thoughts about the subject? (identifies main points)
Are there words or passages which further explain and clarify the general thought? (identifies supporting points)
What main question or questions does the piece raise in your mind?

Can you think of specific cases, incidents, or events that will support the general thoughts or provide answers to the questions? (identifies additional supports)

Key thoughts and questions which emerge from this and the following activity may suggest a thesis, and main and supporting points for the outline which will be written later. Questions may be turned into declarative statements for the outline.

3. Creating a Visual Aid

This activity follows the brainstorming session.

a. Goals of the Visual Aid

To provide a visual aid that comes directly from student interaction and that is created by the students

To give the students an opportunity for the oral expression of thought before a larger group

To provide experience in organizing, clarifying, and expressing ideas in oral delivery

To stimulate additional thought on the topic and generate more ideas from the class as a group

To provide a means for evaluating the students' understanding of the first stage of research

b. Guides for the Visual Aid

Using various colored felt markers and white market paper, each group of students writes and illustrates the topics, questions, and general and particular statements formulated for each subject. These may be mounted on the chalk board or on a wall in the classroom. Each group explains the gist of its discussion and the content of its poster. The class as a group engages in a discussion of each poster. The teacher encourages the class to ask questions like the following which lead to the principles of limiting a subject, formulating research questions, and identifying sources:

Is the subject sufficiently limited?
Does the topic lend itself to research? Why? Why not?
Where can the researcher go for answers to the questions?
Do you have other suggestions for the researcher?

This activity helps the students to define more precisely and clearly the direction their research can take and the method or approach they may use. From the class a student may learn of additional sources or research tactics. For example, perhaps someone in the class knows of a person in the community who faces or has faced the problem or has special experience or knowledge of the problem that a student desires to research. The student may be guided to schedule an interview with this person. Creating a visual aid further stimulates imagination and creativity, and encourages students to write clear, correct sentences and to formulate precise questions. It also combines the written and oral expression of ideas and reinforces points that can be made about the subject.

4. The Plan Sheet

At the end of the foregoing activities, the students hand in a plan sheet for their subjects. This sheet may consist of the following items:

Research Topic _____ (limited)

Research Questions _____

Main Thoughts to Consider _____

Supporting Ideas to Consider _____

Resources to Use _____ (books, magazine articles, letters, interviews, questionnaires, etc.)

The plan sheet provides a final means of evaluation for this stage of research. It may also be used for conferences with students who require individual assistance at this stage.

5. The Research Journal

The students should be encouraged to keep a research journal in which they record their ideas and do daily freewriting exercises about their topics. 10 to 15 minutes of some class sessions may be allotted for freewriting in the journals. From time to time, journal pieces may be read and discussed in class. These should be read to share ideas, not to correct written expression or to discover which is the best paper.

The foregoing activities should stimulate thought and produce a quantity of ideas. Once students focus on *one* idea, they can bring their own perspective and experience to bear. This is the foundation for researching other facts, ideas, and theories, using a variety of sources. The *composing* process can begin only when students' own energy, voice, and creativity are combined with the ideas, experiences, and resources of others.

A Path through the Maze: A Sequential Approach to Writing Documented Papers

Ellen Andrews Knodt, Pennsylvania State University, Ogontz Campus

Any instructor who has assigned a research paper has probably come away from reading 30 (or 60 or 90) final copies realizing that anything which *could* have gone wrong *had*: the papers were almost always "cut and paste jobs" showing the writers' lack of understanding of the subject; quotations were lengthy and had not been selected to support the thesis (if indeed the paper had a clear thesis); the writers' own sentences were sketchy, consisting largely of "And next Mr. Brown said." After my students and I suffered through the research paper several times, I discovered that what they really lacked was practice in the individual skills demanded by the very complex research paper assignment. I had been particularly frustrated by the student who had done all the research work and had copious notes on innumerable 3 x 5 cards but whose paper was incomprehensible. The problem is that writing a research paper or any paper needing documentation requires rather sophisticated techniques of integrating quoted material from several sources with the writer's own words. To complete such an assignment successfully, students must be able to understand their source material, see its relevance to the point they wish to make, extract the quotations which will support their point, introduce or otherwise weave the quotations into their text, and properly punctuate and document the quotation.

To give students practice with each of these skills, I developed a three-step sequence of shorter assignments (500-700 words), building from the simplest to the most complicated tasks involved in writing a documented paper. All of these assignments concern the *writing* of a paper—not the library work involved nor the reading and taking of notes. We are concerned only with what a student can do once he or she has completed the necessary research. The assignments in this sequence do not have to be on the same topic as a research paper, nor, for that matter, does an instructor have to assign a full-fledged research paper.

The first assignment requires the use of quoted material taken from a single source to support a thesis. To provide a link between the students' previous writing about personal experience in their first composition course and their new task of using another's words, I ask them to interview a person and to use notes or tapes of the conversation as the basis for the paper. (Many students I teach own cassette recorders; those who do not have a recorder take notes as accurately as they can.) Since I have been teaching a thematically organized second term English composition course on the American character, my students interview a person at least ten years older than they are on the topic of the democratic ideal. In class, we discuss some questions to ask (drawn from our readings in an anthology and from previous class discussions) and some hints on how to follow up an interesting answer. We are interested in how the interviewed person perceives concepts of democracy such as equality of opportunity, the right to dissent, or the "melting pot." Once students have done their interviews, we discuss how to extract a thesis statement which will capsulize the "interviewee's" attitudes toward the democratic ideal, how to select quotations which will support the thesis, and how to punctuate direct quotations and use paraphrases. We also work with the form of the essay, discussing the purpose of an introduction leading to the thesis, the use of three or four subpoints to develop the thesis, and finally, the possible forms a conclusion could take.

Students seem to like the interview assignment, and it can be modified to fit the theme or subject matter being taught. Other instructors have assigned students to interview someone in an occupation that the student intends to pursue, and then to write an essay analyzing the advantages and disadvantages of that occupation. Or students could choose a controversial issue like the death penalty, gun control legislation, or the legalization of marijuana; interview someone on his views, and then write an essay explaining that person's position on the issue.

Whatever the topic, students seem to learn some very important basic research writing skills from this interview assignment. In order to write the paper, students must be able to sift through the person's conversation to find quotations to support a thesis, and then fit the quotations into the text of the paper by providing introductions to or comments on them. They must also know the mechanics of punctuating quotations correctly. Because the source is another person rather than a published work, students can concentrate on the task of thesis and support without the added difficulties of reading and understanding published material. And because students are using only one source, the "interviewee," they avoid the problem of interweaving quotations from several different sources and of footnoting and documenting them.

The second assignment in the sequence requires students to support a thesis by using material from two published primary sources. In addition to the previous tasks, this assignment requires that the students read and understand published material, develop a thesis from that material, and select quotations from both sources to support the thesis. At this point, too, the students learn how to footnote quotations taken from our text (the source of the material for this assignment). This second step, then, moves the students from using a first-hand account (the interview) to the more complex task of using two published sources.

Topics for this paper are about success in America and usually take the form of a comparison or contrast like "Compare blue-collar attitudes toward work with white-collar attitudes toward work as seen in two essays in our text" or "Analyze the values held by the main characters in the stories by John Cheever and Harvey Swados." An instructor could assign a topic requiring library work for this paper, but the number of sources used should be limited to reduce the complexity of the task. For example, the instructor might ask the students to read two magazine articles on water pollution and do an analysis or evaluation of the articles, using direct quotations for support. Or students could be assigned to read two short stories by an author, derive a thesis based on their reading, and write a paper supporting their thesis with relevant quotations.

The last assignment in the three-step sequence is the most difficult. For this paper students must use at least three sources, at least one of which must be from literary criticism. Since criticism is usually the most difficult material for students to read and interpret and since students must use a greater number of sources in this paper, this assignment poses the greatest complexity. In addition to continuing their work on footnoting, students also learn to do a bibliography for this assignment. I usually control the source of critical material by mimeographing passages from several texts, but one could also use a casebook containing critical commentary or assign library work for this assignment. Topics for these papers are derived from some concept found in the critical material and then verified or disproven by material taken from the primary works. For example, a critical comment on Hemingway's style of writing might be supported by reference to a novel and short story or several short stories.

Students feel more confident about beginning a full-scale research project after completing this series of shorter assignments. To be sure, they have to cope with the frustrations of finding the information and the task of taking notes on what they read, but the job of sifting the important information from the unimportant, arranging quotations to support a thesis, fitting quotes into the texts of their papers (without dominating the texts), and documenting the quotations properly has been simplified because they have practiced all these skills on shorter, more manageable assignments. For students who have never done a documented paper, or who have been left to flounder without instruction on how to proceed, this three-step sequence may provide a path through the maze.

3 About Teaching Writing: Revising and Editing

Careful revising and editing are essential but often overlooked steps in writing. Students who become proficient at proofreading and revising their work save teachers time and effort. The authors of the articles in this chapter, realizing the necessity for teaching students how to revise and edit, suggest color coding to help students establish organization, advise use of groups for revising and proofreading activities, and provide guidelines for instructing students in proofreading and revision.

Color Coding and Other Devices for Teaching Organization

Helen Thompson, South Newton Junior High School,
Kentland, Indiana

"Lo! thy dread empire, Chaos! is restor'd;
Light dies before thy uncreating word;
Thy hand, great Anarch! lets the curtain fall,
And universal darkness buries all."

Alexander Pope, *The Dunciad*,
Bk. iv. 1. 653

Anyone endeavoring to teach theme writing will most likely recognize the truth of the above quotation. Chaos has extended to the writing of themes at the secondary level. Organization of thought, and to an even greater extent organization of these ideas on paper, often seem to be a lost art. I have devised a method for teaching theme organization and for promoting careful copy-reading and rewrite that might prove helpful to others teaching these basic skills.

Former students of my structured writing class who have attended colleges and universities have reported most favorably on the results of the method. For the first time in six years of teaching I feel that I have progressed in teaching students to write accurately and in an organized manner.

The method? Really quite simple—but different: I begin with a very arbitrary structure requirement for outlining the theme and for writing the opening paragraph of the theme. I prepare and distribute a list of the essential items on an outline form; they are: introductory material, thesis statement, main points, supporting points, and conclusion. Essential items for the opening paragraph are: attention-getting sentence or sentences, background material, topic sentences, and thesis statement.

I'm sure that the reader is thinking at this point that there is nothing new or different about this. The difference comes, however, as I begin showing the student how to determine if all necessary components of the opening paragraph are included and if the theme is organized correctly. I use color coding to establish organization and relationships. The student is instructed to make an outline on a form which I provide and to write an opening paragraph following specific directions. These must be an attention-getting sentence, some background material, at least two topic sentences (which must correspond with the main points specified on the outline) and a thesis statement as the concluding sentence of the opening paragraph. Students usually progress this far relatively easily—not necessarily correctly, but easily. At this point I ask them to take color markers and do a bit of underlining. The attention-getter is to be underlined in red. (All coding is open to teacher's choice.) The background material is underlined in green, topic sentences in yellow, the thesis statement in black, and, to show a relationship with topic sentences, main points on the outline are underlined in yellow.

As the underlining begins, problems and questions arise: "I don't seem to have anything to underline in yellow in my opening paragraph ... I can't find anything to underline in black—what is a thesis statement? ... My main points don't correspond to my topic sentences ... What is background material? I can't find anything to underline in green." Students must find for themselves the components of the opening paragraph, determine that they have both topic sentences and corresponding main points underlined in matching yellow, and must underline a firm thesis statement in black at the end of the opening paragraph; the necessity of pinpointing specifics in color soon shows either the presence or absence of these items.

After completing the underlining, showing me both the outline and the color-coded opening paragraph, and making any necessary changes, the student proceeds with the writing of the first draft of the theme. Again, using the same color-code system, the markers are used to underline the attention-getting sentence, the background material, the topic sentences and the thesis statement in the first paragraph, and the main points where these appear in the body of the theme. The themes, with outlines stapled at the back, are collected and I attach a critique sheet to the front. The critique sheet has a section at the top designed for scoring organization and a section at the bottom for scoring errors in punctuation, spelling, and grammar. There is also provision for recording vocabulary errors, such as use of improper word for meaning intended, but I do not use this section when students are critiquing.

The class is divided into groups of three and each group is given three themes with instructions to read each theme aloud, fill in the top (organization) part of the score sheet as a joint effort, and then work individually with the themes to score the bottom portion of the sheet. Each student scores a different section for each theme, i.e. one student copyreads for spelling errors on one theme, punctuation errors on a second, and grammatical errors on the third. Errors are marked in red, and the total number of errors of a particular type is entered in the appropriate blank on the critique sheet, along with the recording students' signature. After this score card is completed the themes are returned to students for rewrite. Then the complete assembly is turned in— outline, rough draft, critique score card, and rewritten theme. As I grade the final effort I check any error I find against the critique sheet and the rough draft; if the student copyreader has missed this error, he or she is penalized as well as the author of the theme.

When using this teaching method with students who have a great deal of trouble recognizing the topic sentence–main point relationship, I use a skit to demonstrate the connection. After choosing a theme which has a clear representation of the correspondence of the topic sentences in the opening paragraph and the main points in the theme, I make placards which read: Mr. Attention-Getter, Miss Background, Mrs. Topic Sentence One, Mrs. Topic Sentence Two, Mr. Thesis Statement, Miss Main Point One and Miss Main Point Two. These are arbitrary designations. The specific requirement is that the topic sentence–main point character relationship must be direct: parent-child, aunt or uncle- niece or nephew. Each character reads certain lines from the theme and the other students listen to determine if the writer of the theme has given the characters the proper lines to say, listening especially for that relationship between the topic sentence in the opening paragraph and its main point. Even advanced students participate in this activity enthusiastically, and it does provide a slight diversion from everyday teaching tactics.

The teaching process described has proved to be a most effective way of directing students toward good organization and careful observation of proper mechanics in theme writing. I feel, also, that better content in the theme occurs as a result of this demand for organization, since the student must put into the theme the ideas which the organization has dictated and must omit extraneous material which careful organization shows to be unnecessary.

Composition:
Competitive or Cooperative?

Richard E. Barbieri, Milton Academy, Milton, Massachusetts

"But sir, you can't keep us from grade-grubbing. That's the American way." I guess it is, especially in a high-powered college prep school like the one where I teach. Through the years I had seen enough of the conflict and animosity generated by the quest for grades. Competition had been bred into these students from early childhood, by sports, by parents' career models, and by constant pressure for admission to the "best" schools at every rung up the ladder. Therefore, cooperation was a basic skill as necessary to them as literacy, or more so. But was it possible to promote both simultaneously, to instill cooperation amid the necessary individualism of composition?

The plan jelled slowly, nurtured by reading Charity James, comparing students' teamwork in sports and activities with their egocentricity in English class, hearing of cooperative techniques used in Chinese education, and most of all by attending an NCTE workshop on "Human Values in the English Classroom." At last I felt ready to try the experiment.

I had two major aims: to improve the students' ability to work together, and to apply these improved cooperative skills to the task of revising compositions. Evaluation would be both personal, in the form of frequent discussions and written critiques by the class, and academic, in my grading of the papers.

The first step was to find a suitable writing topic. Too narrow an assignment would blur the distinction between cooperation and plagiarism; too open a subject risked leaving no room for mutual comprehension and cooperation. Therefore, I based the composition on a story we were reading, Graham Greene's "The Destructors," so that everyone would begin on a common footing, but I tried to avoid the traditional critical essay, which would reinforce familiar hierarchies of "good" and "bad" students. The topic was:

> Toward the end of "The Destructors" Blackie and Trevor [the
> story's two main characters] are sitting together. Blackie sug-
> gests that Trevor must really hate Mr. Thomas [the old man
> whose house the boys are wrecking], but Trevor replies "All
> this hate and love, it's soft, it's hooey. There's only things,
> Blackie."
>
> Respond to Trevor's statement. You may explain why you
> think he feels that way, or you may talk about whether you
> think what he says is true, or what you think it means. The only
> requirement is that you use his words as a jumping-off point
> for your own reflections on the story or on life as you see it.

After collecting the assignment I set it aside until the next phase
of the sequence was completed.

To make the class aware of the need for cooperation, and to let
them practice it in a nonthreatening environment, I used a
number of group exercises, most of them from Stanford and
Stanford's *Learning Discussion Skills Through Games* (Citation
Press, 1969). Among the more exciting of these are the "Lost on
the Moon" game and the "Bank Robbery Mystery." In the former,
students are asked to rank fifteen items in order of usefulness to a
lunar landing party stranded 200 miles from its base camp. First
each person makes an individual written choice, then the class
discusses the list and arrives at a consensus. In theory, and almost
always in practice, the consensus list is more accurate (by comparison with NASA's ranking) than that of any one individual. (It
worked out that way for us in all but one instance, where a
student knew a crucial fact but didn't tell it to the group, thus
lowering their score and showing in reverse the value of teamwork.) In the "Bank Robbery Mystery," students are each given
one or more clues (depending on class size) to a crime, and must
agree on the criminal, the method, and the motive by discussing
the evidence, without collecting or otherwise physically passing
the clues. A time clock and subsequent discussion show how well
the group worked together.

Before the exercises began I explained that we would be
working for several days on cooperative techniques, and that we
would conclude with a graded assignment based on cooperation.
After each exercise we talked at length about what had helped or
hindered the group and who had made the greatest contributions.
The class quickly realized that cooperation produced more success for everyone than individualistic wrangling, and they showed
great perception in choosing—usually unanimously—the most
helpful members of the group. These did not always turn out to be

the usual "stars" of the class, a fact that became more significant as the sequence continued.

After several meetings devoted to such exercises and discussions, we moved to the compositions. Having made three copies of each paper, I divided the class into groups of four. Each member of the group received a copy of the four papers written by his or her group. These papers had no marks; I kept all my grades and comments in a separate notebook. I then outlined the procedure to be followed.

Each group was to have two class days, plus assignment time, to work together revising and editing the papers. I would then assign a grade to each group—the same for every member—based not on how good the papers were, but on how much each had improved from the first version. I made it clear that I would be looking for general improvement in the group, so that slight progress on all four papers would count for more than great improvement in one or two and no change in the others. I suggested three principles for revision:

1. Find out what the other students want to say and help them say it more effectively.

2. Don't ask them to change what they were trying to say unless it seems absolutely necessary and unless you can persuade them of the necessity.

3. Help each other correct mechanical errors, but make this only one aspect of the revision, not the whole thing.

Over the next two days I moved around the room, listening to the groups work. Each had its distinctive tone. Some approached the job ruthlessly. In others, one or more members were defensive, unwilling to accept advice or to criticize. Frequently the proportion of praise to criticism was, to my ear, too low. Yet they made progress. Some students groped tentatively for the kind way to phrase a suggestion: "I don't know, but I think it would be better this way." Others learned to begin with the compliment that disarms defensiveness and makes constructive criticism acceptable. Many were frank in suggesting that a paper read as if it had been rushed, and elicited admissions teachers never hear. As one person said in the final critique, "When your friends tell you something is wrong it's different than hearing it from the teacher."

Two patterns particularly stood out. The stronger the students, the less well the groups worked. Successful writers clashed, and by their assertiveness often dragged others in wrong directions.

On the other hand, weaker students grasped at the chance for improvement, listened to each other closely, sought times to work after class, and were more sensitive to each other's feelings and quicker to leap to someone's defense.

Second, some groups focused almost entirely on matters of editing, improving the papers' mechanics but ignoring larger issues of style, organization, or approach. Major change, it seemed, was too threatening for some even to suggest. In one group, on the other hand, a student had taken what to me was an original and exciting approach to the topic, but two other group members, not really understanding what he was up to, attacked him vigorously, producing first strong resistance, then sullen capitulation. I was sorely tempted to intervene, but forced myself to keep clear, watching the group fall apart through dissension and hoping that the experience would prove valuable for them, if not now, at least in retrospect.

Grading the papers (grades ranged from A to C) I found significant improvement in a little over half, a better proportion than I had usually found when students worked independently. Further, there was a clear correlation between cooperation in a group during the classes and progress on the papers. Those who had struck off in their own directions accomplished little compared to those who had worked together.

After returning the papers and discussing them, I asked everyone to submit a detailed anonymous evaluation of the whole project. The responses were gratifyingly positive, making me feel that more had probably been gained in personal than academic respects. Rating the whole sequence, 26% described their feelings as Very Good, 68% as Good, 5% as Fair, and none as Poor or Very Poor. On the writing component the scores were 5% Very Good, 67% Good, and 28% Fair. Asked "How much did this exercise help your writing?" 67% replied A Fair Amount and 33% A Little (no one chose either Very Much or Not At All). Finally, 60% thought their group had worked together Well or Very Well, 18% described their group's behavior as Okay, and only 12% thought they had worked Rather Badly.

Replies to the open-ended questions interested me even more. To the question "What changes, if any, have you noticed in yourself as a result of the sequence?" students made such replies as: "I think that now I will not just give my ideas, but will listen to others." "I am more able to adjust my opinions to those of someone else whose reasoning seems more logical than mine." In response to the same question asked about the class as a whole, students cited such changes as "better organization," more listening and consideration," "more unity as a group," "more opinions coming from many more people," and "We don't yell as much. We've learned it won't help the discussion." But there's a pessimist in every crowd: "We are openly starting to hate each other," suggested one critic.

Other questions also showed people recognizing the benefits of cooperation. Asked what changes should be made in the class's behavior, almost half hoped for less arguing and stubbornness, and suggested the need for more open-mindedness, cooperation, concentration, organization, and acceptance of others' opinions. The pervasiveness of the effect was shown by answers to the question "Who helped you the most in revising?" Here almost two-thirds of the students in the class were mentioned on at least one questionnaire.

The good effects of the sequence lasted, by my own observations, well after the conclusion of the experiment, and in one case proved especially durable and important. One boy—I'll call him Jim—had a record of mild dyslexia and attendant emotional problems. In class Jim was hypersensitive and totally lacking in confidence, facts that he tried to conceal behind a facade of humorous put-downs of his own work and abilities. But during the exercise it became apparent both to him and to the class that despite his problems with spelling and mechanics he had a great facility for problem-solving and for leadership. In the games he was again and again cited as "most helpful," and of all the groups his had the best record of improvement. From then on his confidence improved markedly, and so did his work, culminating in his selection as a major sportswriter and editor on the school paper. Setting aside the general benefits of the experiment, the change in Jim alone would have made the program a worthwhile innovation.

Managing a Proofreading Dialogue

Thomas D. Gillett, East Junior–Senior High School,
Rochester, New York

It has always amazed me how a fairly competent high school junior can master usage exercises, correctly spell and use difficult words, and punctuate a wide variety of sentence structures when these challenges arise in their own contexts (grammar exercises, spelling quizzes), but will fail miserably when applying exactly the same exercises to the writing of his or her own compositions. I had never realized the size of the gap between writing theory and practice until a budding E. B. White timorously approached my desk clutching his latest effort which had been red-pen "corrected" so copiously that it looked as if it had seen duty as a pressure bandage for a serious abrasion. He pointed to the two-inch high letters "PROOFREAD!" which bannered his paper; "I don't know how to do this," he confessed.

This epiphanic episode led me to develop a strategy for teaching proofreading as a basic skill in a composition class. The student mentioned above was not atypical; few students, in fact, can evaluate their own work for clarity, coherence, and mechanical accuracy. But self-evaluation and self-correction form the *foundation* of good writing. If the *writer* cannot accomplish a cogent analysis of a piece, writing is likely to be a hit or miss proposition at best. The process I now use incorporates peer evaluation, comprehensive proofreading, class participation, and attention to the individual student.

I presently organize my composition course (of tenth through twelfth graders) to encourage the development of self-evaluation and proofreading skills. In many ways, it is like composition courses have always been: students write one essay each week, usually of 300-600 words; each week's assignment focuses on a particular technique for developing an idea (e.g., examples, compare/contrast, definition, process analysis); examples of each week's technique are distributed and discussed; numerous short assignments—reading and writing—supplement the weekly assignments.

The variation in the traditional writing course comes in the way student essays are used to reinforce principles of good writing. First, I make abundant corrections, criticisms, and commendations on each paper. I then extract a sentence or two from each paper to share with the class via the overhead projector. One or two class periods are devoted to the group's analyzing these "gems"—anonymously, of course. For example, an essay assignment using the technique of comparison/contrast yielded these:

> When you get to high school, you find that kids there are divided into two groups, the honor students and the athletes.
>
> The honor student and the athlete, one is a book finatic, the other is a sport finatic.
>
> In life, people genrally find that with every person they meet, they have common and conflicting interests. The Honor Student and the Athlete, although different in many ways, also share some similarities.
>
> Both the honor student and the athlete have one thing in common, and that is reaching a goal.

For some strange, unexplainable reason, students are better able to criticize individual sentences when the overhead flicks on and the sentence glows on the projection screen. In the first two examples above, students easily identified the problems (after unanimously agreeing that the first was clearer and more coherent): both generalize and need qualification; the second is a run-on with misspellings. The third sentence was universally acclaimed as a lucid, expressive opener for a composition. The final example was scored for being vague and unnecessarily restrictive. The analysis of these four sentences involved lengthy discussion and took most of a class period.

Many sentences I select for viewing are evaluated and corrected by students saying, "It doesn't make sense (or "sound right"); it would be better if it said...." And in most cases, the correction offered is a valid improvement over the projected example. Some sentences from the same assignment as above which fell into the "doesn't-sound-good" class:

> Films come in black and white and color. Many fancy tricks can be accomplished with a movie camera.
>
> This composition will show the likeness and difference of stage acting and film acting.

A stage play requires human time and effort.

In the realm of visual entertainment, the two most prominent forms, the stage play and the film, are bitter rivals.

Fear and courage are related to each other, because they are both facing up to reality.

It is essential that this exercise not be directed toward identifying and labeling incorrect or awkward constructions. If the aim is to teach writing, the emphasis must be on the skill of rewriting the unclear sentence or restating the poorly worded phrase. As students become comfortable with this process, it begins to be a natural part of their own writing procedure.

Students do provide examples in their writing of all the major, recurring composition errors. From a semester's work, I have selected some of the more frequent afflictions:

wrong word:	Many kids forget their hunger and *capitulate* their vegetables over to the next table.
clichés:	You've just got to keep your eyes peeled.
	He knows where he's going and where he's coming from.
fragment:	Something which not everyone else has, patience.
convoluted sentences:	Another example of another country's way of greeting is the country Steponfeete's.
	To start off in my opinion as a female and who is for Women's Liberation to an extent, both sexes have their weaker points.
unclear pronouns:	Ridiculous as it may sound, it can be thought of as a move in the right direction.
distracting repetition:	One thing that they all have in common which is more common than the common cold, is boredom.
faulty logic:	She is a machine that never tires. But she tires now.
	If you walk down the corridor of a school, it is plain to see that males try to show off their muscles. This only goes to show that girls are stronger.
colloquial usage:	Sometimes the concerned parent is just too much.

unwarranted use of choppy sentences:	When I step on that bus, I know what I am going to see. I am going to see the typical bus driver.
parallel structure:	They don't know whether it will be warmer or will it stay cold?

The collection of weekly "highlight" sentences has been labeled "The Good, the Bad, and the Ugly" by my class, and, though they feel I emphasize the "bad" and the "ugly," I consciously include sentences which are examples of good writing: clear topic statements; coherent, complex sentences; particularly appropriate word choices.

Among the benefits of this procedure is a higher level of involvement by individual students. Because *everyone* is represented, students seem more willing to be attentive, watching for their own "good" or "ugly." Because all the examples are drawn from responses to the same assignment, class members have a general familiarity with what each writer was attempting; all examples have a common context. This familiarity invites self-evaluation by comparing and contrasting: "My paragraph would have been clearer had I organized it like that." Because the selections are offered without "credit" to the author, students are less threatened by the peer criticism. In fact, when I ask the class what could be improved in a sentence, the "author" is often the first to offer a reconstruction. Because only a sentence or two is taken from each essay, no student need feel oppressed by the criticism. An added benefit of this practice is that students begin to develop the habit of looking at their own work sentence by sentence. Generally, students seem to enjoy the classes devoted to their own triumphs and errors.

For the teacher, the procedure engenders class discussion in a class where discussions are sometimes difficult to manage. The short samples to be considered allow immediate analysis. The group sessions provide the teacher with one more source of information for determining whether or not the students are learning anything.

Student reaction to the practice offers a fitting conclusion. On leaving the class last semester, a young writer, in typical teenage fashion, gave praise in the form of faint damnation: "I used to be able to really shovel it on essay tests—now I feel uncomfortable when I write something that says nothing, even if it sounds great." I like to think that meant he learned something in my course.

Profitable Proofreading

S. Kenneth Benson, Pacific Union College, Angwin, California

When thoughts tumble forward faster than pen or typewriter can handle, errors invariably creep in during the early stages of writing. Even the most experienced writers need to proofread their final drafts for careless errors. If you can get these concepts across to your students, proofreading becomes an accepted part of the writing process. I sometimes tell students, "When you write, forget about punctuation, spelling, sentences, and the like if they hinder your thinking process. Get down on paper what you want to communicate. After you have your thoughts down on paper and corrected for basic content, then worry about the mechanics. Now read it several times. If you are a poor speller, read every word carefully for spelling. Then proofread for fragments, run-ons, and the like. Don't be satisfied with one or two readings; you may have to proofread six or more times!"

When the students come to class with what they think is the finished composition, I ask them to proofread the theme at least twice more before turning it in. I reserve about thirty minutes of class time to answer questions on proofreading. I will spell words, read individual sentences for completeness and punctuation; however, the student must have a particular point in mind. Some teachers might object to this help, but I am so elated to have students question spelling and other problems in mechanics that I give as much help as possible. After all, what is the goal in proofreading? Don't we want them to read their own themes with a critical eye?

Before the first theme, we go over the correction symbols I use. Usually we also do one or two worksheets on common proofreading errors and major sentence problems. The interest in proofreading is understandably minimal at this point.

When the themes are returned, correction symbols have been placed on the left side of the page. The right side is reserved for problems in content. A one-page grading scale is attached to the end of the paper that evaluates both mechanics and content. If a theme receives a grade lower than a C, it should be revised completely. However, everyone revises proofreading errors, not to change the grade of the theme, but as an exercise in proof-reading.

The method I developed to make students pay attention to proof-reading symbols was an act of desperation. For years I tried correcting the mechanical errors on the papers and perhaps having the student recopy the theme. This procedure seldom helped the mechanics on the next theme. Next, I tried using correction symbols on the left margin of each line and asking students to read them when the themes were returned. This did not improve mechanics *or* get students interested in proofreading. In both methods, the teacher learns about the students' problems, but students do not. Finally, I struck upon this idea.

On a prescribed day, all students are to bring their last themes to class. On the board I write these directions:

1. On the left margin of your original theme, number the first ten correction symbols consecutively, 1 through 10. (This sounds simple, but you soon find that students do not listen and follow directions very well.)
2. Take a new piece of paper and put your name on it. Using the same numbers as you just placed on the left margins of your theme, you are now to correct the first ten errors.
3. If the error is spelling, write SP after the number on your correction page and spell the word correctly.
4. For all other errors, study the problem carefully. Copy the entire sentence that had an error, but make the needed correction. After this, explain in your own words why a correction symbol was placed on the left margin of that line.

From then on, my time is spent answering individual students on errors they do not understand. I circulate around the room, or they come to my desk. (Suggest they correct the errors they do understand first, then they can ask several questions at once.) It may be hectic at first, and a teacher-aide can be very helpful at this time. Perhaps some of your better students can help. The main value is to have students correcting their own errors and learning the specific reasons for the corrections.

On the following page is the title and one paragraph of a returned theme.

Student Theme

1 2 3
C P Awk   Trying to get acquainted with a new roompartner can be
            frustrating

4   It can be difficult to assert yourself when your new
Awk   roompartner does not realize what he does that annoys you.
            As the two of you progress in organizing the room, your
            roompartner may make a few decisions of his own. For
            example, my roompartner and I talked about our floor being
5   cold when we get up in the morning and how nice it would
P   be to have a rug. After class one day, I walked into our room
6   and there was this carpet; old, moist, and had the smell of
Not para.   mildew. Jim, my roompartner, was still trimming the edges
7   of the carpet. He explained to me that he found it behind
P   Dean Smiths house. It was difficult for me to try to tell him
            that I would not tolerate it. As I did try to tell him this, I
            failed in getting my point across. Many times I would try to
            tell him, "We will dispose of it when we get tired of it." He
            got the wrong impression and said, "How could we ever get
            tired of it? Remember how cold the floor was!" Jim bothers
            me in other ways too. Many times Jim cleaned up the room.
8   As he did he misplaced my belongings, so that I could not
Awk   find them, and this would annoy me. Everytime I tried to
            talk about the new arrangement of my belongings, he would
            ask what I thought about the cleanliness of the room. I said,
            "It is fine." But in my mind I would try to forget about it.
            My politeness and sensitivity toward his feelings kept me
9   from getting my point across. Just the chance of breaking a
Awk   friendship bothered me and this is why people do not speak
10   exactly what they mean, for fear it would hurt the new
Pro. Ante. acquaintance. And this is the frustrating part about it.

The student correction page(s) are stapled to the front of the theme. If the corrections are well done, they can be corrected quickly. Occasionally you may have to look at the theme to straighten out some special difficulty. For example, sometimes the student changes the wrong word for a spelling error.

Student Corrections

1,2,3. Getting Acquainted With a New Roommate
    Capitalize all major words in a title. Do not capitalize short prepositions and articles unless they are the first word. Do not underline original titles. Underline only names of books, etc.
    The title was too long and awkward. "Roommate" is more common than "roompartner."

4. It can be difficult to assert yourself when your roommate does not realize that he annoys you.

The sentence had too many words like "when," "what," and "that;" I simplified the sentence.

5, 6. After class one day, I walked into our room, and there was this carpet—old, moist, and smelly with mildew.

There should have been a comma after "room" because it is a compound sentence.

I should not have used a semi-colon after "carpet" because what comes after it is not a sentence. A colon or a dash introduces these adjectives coming after the noun; "had the smell of mildew" is not parallel with the two adjectives.

7. He explained to me that he found it behind Dean Smith's house.

"Smith's" is singular possessive.

8. He annoyed me when he misplaced my belongings where I could not find them.

The sentence was too long and involved. I simplified it.

9. The chance of breaking our friendship bothered me. I suppose this is why many people do not speak frankly with a new friend.

The original sentence was too long and involved.

10. Being unable to speak openly with my new roommate is frustrating.

The sentence was vague; the antecedent for "it" is vague also.

The students may have trouble with the corrections. For example, they may not quite remember the rules for the possessive. You can either teach on the spot, or you can refer them to the handbook. I prefer to teach or review the item with the students if they are concerned enough to ask. Usually if you remind them of the rules, they understand, especially if you have done some groundwork before the first theme. However, you may have to reteach some points several times for some students. I handle this exercise as a separate daily grade, not as part of the theme grade. If twenty points are given for the exercise, then each item is worth two points. Unless the student gives reasons for the errors (except for spelling), no credit is given. If the correction is not clear, no credit is given for that item either. If the students get more than one or two wrong, they can redo the paper. On the second correction, they write on the same paper by adding rules or making changes. The most common error is failing to give the reason for the correction.

The goal of this method is to have students proofread their themes before they pass them in. From my experience, most students read much more carefully after they have corrected one or two themes. This may be due to a genuine interest in proof-reading or a distaste for correcting the theme. Whatever the reason, students tend to proofread more carefully before submitting themes. This method also gives the teacher an opportunity to do a lot of individualized teaching on proofreading material that is relevant to the student.

Revision: A Basic Skill

Marylyn E. Calabrese, Tredyffrin/Easttown School District, Berwyn, Pennsylvania

"Do I have to do it over?"

Most students in writing classes hate to revise. Some see it as frustrating busywork; others view it as painstaking drudgery. Most do not understand why or how their writing needs redoing. Actually, revising should be exciting, challenging work. It can even be fun. Finding the right word, cutting four paragraphs into two, rearranging the order of a sentence to give more emphasis, editing, proofreading, and recopying—all of these activities should be an integral part of every writing program, with special strategies and lessons designed to make them productive and rewarding to the learner.

Teaching revision increases verbal competency and helps to bring about conscientious work habits; it may even foster in students a fascination with the dynamics of language. It also means teaching pride in one's work, in excellence of verbal expression, and above all, in the expectation of and commitment to doing one's best. In my classroom, I often compare it to the preparations necessary in giving a speech, taking part in a play, or competing on a sports team. Revising is a form of practice. It is rare that we are satisfied with our first attempts.

A writing program with a serious commitment to revision should include a consideration of these basic questions:

1. Who decides what needs to be revised?

2. Are the critical comments and suggestions for revision clear, specific, and thorough?

3. What choices in methods of revision does the student have available?

4. Is sufficient time allotted in conferences so that students can ask questions about their revisions?

5. What followup measures are provided so that teacher and student can keep a record of the progress of the originals and revisions?

1. *Who Decides What Needs to Be Revised?*

In addition to the teacher-critic, the use of the student-critic can enlarge the range of critical feedback. Students often respond favorably to critical comments from their peers if done in a positive and constructive atmosphere. One method is to have each composition critiqued separately by several students, each one making notes on a separate sheet of paper. Without looking at the other critiques, the teacher reviews the compositions and adds additional suggestions. Usually there is considerable overlap in the kinds of comments offered and the student feels part of a group endeavor, rather than the target of a teacher/student one-way dialogue.

2. *Are the Critical Comments and Suggestions for Revision Clear, Specific, and Thorough?*

"Third paragraph unclear—revise." "Needs further development—rewrite."

Receiving a paper with these kinds of incomplete comments can be very frustrating to the student writer. And the reverse situation, can be just as discouraging—a paper overwhelmed with red marks and notations. A balanced approach will include enough specifics without confusing the student. A good way to judge the suitability of the comments is by the kinds of questions students ask. Are they able to revise on the basis of the comments or do they need additional examples? Very often, a student learns by having very detailed comments on a few papers in the beginning of the course, and then just simple directions on the remaining compositions. It is important to remember that the quality of the revision may be only as good as the quality of the critical comments and suggestions on the original paper. Any teacher who expects a thorough rewrite (where it is necessary) will need to take the time to do a thorough critique of the paper. If nothing else, this kind of attention will convey to the student the importance of a thorough revision.

What is a thorough revision? Does every paper need to be totally redone?

3. *What Choices in Methods of Revision Does the Student Have Available?*

Redoing every part of every paper can be a deadly exercise in overkill. On the other hand, the total revision of a few compositions with complete instructions and guidance can be invaluable lessons in writing. Depending on the nature of the writing problem, a *part* of the paper can be redone, perhaps several key paragraphs. A student can use a numbering system to indicate the errors on the original composition along with the corresponding corrections on a separate sheet. This approach works well with a combination of spelling, punctuation, and usage errors in a paper where the basic organization and substance are sound. These kinds of shortcuts to revision aid both students and teachers so that time can be spent reworking difficult passages rather than recopying entire papers for only a few minor errors.

4. *Is Sufficient Time Allotted in Conferences for Students to Ask Questions about Their Revisions?*

If students are to do an efficient job of revising, there must be time for conferences with the teacher. Scheduling conferences with each student is difficult for teachers with large classes and a full teaching schedule, but it is essential if students are expected to spend considerable time in efficient revision. Extensive individual conferences during class time after the first few assignments can provide the necessary groundwork for shorter future conferences.

Individual student-teacher conferences are not the only way to deal with questions pertaining to revision. One time-saving alternative is to have students assist each other in answering questions and starting on revision. This reduces their dependency on the teacher, and increases their understanding of the writing of their peers. When paired with those of different writing abilities, students are often surprised to find that in helping others revise their papers, they have gained a new perspective on approaching their own.

5. *What Followup Measures are Provided So That Teacher and Student Can Keep a Record of the Progress of the Originals and Revisions?*

What happens to the completed revisions? This is a key question. Revision can best be accomplished in a structured writing program that includes individual needs assessment, the setting of objectives for the individual and for the total group, and the monitoring and evaluation of these efforts. An individual progress chart might include writing needs and problem areas, a checklist to record common writing errors, and a structure to monitor the progress of the revised papers. Asking students to go back and periodically read over their writing folders, including both originals and revisions, helps them to view their writing progress as a whole. Students need to see that their revisions are an integral part of their entire writing program.

One final note.

The more involvement and purpose students feel in their writing, the more likely they are to expend the extra energy it takes to revise, refine, and polish the final drafts. Topics drawn from experience rather than from textbooks lend themselves to this kind of effort; for example, if the final product is something that the students will actually use or send, then the need for revision is built in. Letters to the editors of local newspapers, letters of introduction to school guidance counselors, autobiographical essays that form part of a student's application for college admission all obviously need to be revised until "publishable." Other "real" audiences for student work include high school newspapers, students in other schools, and also classroom newspapers. In short, writing for publication gives students an excellent incentive to make their writing as good as it possibly can be.

In summary, the teaching of revision as a basic skill is as integral a part of a writing program as is paragraph organization, sentence structure, and word usage. The student who is expected to revise, taught how to do it with clear and specific directions, and given classroom time for writing conferences, will complain less about "doing it over" and is more likely to request another opportunity of getting it "just right." Some may even find a great improvement in their basic writing skills.

4 About Teaching Punctuation, Grammar, and Spelling

There are those who would assert that the mechanics of writing are superficial, that it's *what* you say that's important. Yes, what you say *is* the most important aspect of writing, but mechanics are far from superficial if they are the means of getting what you say across to the reader. Some of the finer points of punctuation, spelling, and grammar (specifically, sentence combining and sentence modeling) are approached here with the student, not the textbook, in mind. Hints for individualizing instruction and making learning fun ease the task of teaching these necessary skills.

Build a Skill, Step by Step

Doris Master, Board of Cooperative Educational Services, Nassau County, New York

Readers of a publication such as this need not be convinced of the need for providing elementary school children with the requisite skills for the fluent and accurate recording of their ideas. These skills must include enough knowledge of punctuation to make students comfortable with its use. Effective writing means making the reader feel and understand what the writer feels and understands. Punctuation is essential to this process. I would like to describe a technique I used to teach my fourth graders the use of quotation marks in writing dialogue. The treatment of the particular skill demonstrates the sequence I followed; it could easily be adapted to teach other skills as well.

I selected a number of children who had attempted to use quotation marks in their writing, and who no longer needed help in writing simple, complete sentences. By limiting the group to those who wrote sentences freely and correctly, I was able to limit my instruction to the one specific skill; a skill which the children recognized had given them difficulty. I reminded the children that they had had trouble reading their own and each other's work because they could not determine which character said what. I then "invited" them to join the "Quotation Mark Seminar." Of course, these highly motivated writers enthusiastically remained in the small group with me.

Our first lesson in the Seminar consisted of a discussion of comic strips and how the author and artist indicated the exact words of a character. I drew a figure on the board and enclosed exciting phrases in balloons emanating from the mouths of the cartoon characters. We discussed the feasibility of doing this in our written work, and the children agreed that it would not work. I then explained very carefully how punctuation marks were used in direct quotations. We made up funny or exciting statements for the cartoon characters on the board and punctuated them together. The students' first assignment was to find a three-frame

90

comic strip, paste it on paper, and rewrite the conversation in the balloons using quotation marks. The children completed this easily and shared their work with each other. The next day I assigned some pages from an English textbook dealing with direct and indirect quotations. We discussed them and completed and corrected the exercises. The following assignment sent the children to their writing folders for some of their own work to correct. They were told to look through their papers to find some writing which contained conversation and to rewrite it correctly. If their own writing did not contain dialogue, they were encouraged to use dialogue from their classmates' writing. The children found this a little more difficult to do, but after discussing *what* they were trying to communicate, and after consulting with their small group and me, most of them wrote a few lines of conversation and punctuated them correctly.

For the next step, I displayed pictures which showed two or more people in varied circumstances. One picture showed a man and a young boy looking into a hospital nursery at a nurse displaying three newborn babies. Another picture showed two stuffed animals hugging each other. Yet another showed boys with hot dogs and baseball equipment. Several other pictures were also available. The children were told to choose one picture which appealed to them and to decide what the characters were saying to each other. I urged them to make the conversation revealing enough to explain what had happened before and possibly what might happen next. The children wrote authentic, realistic dialogue, and all but one of the eight children used the punctuation marks correctly. I spoke with the child having difficulty, and gave her a few dittos to help her recognize direct and indirect quotations. Then she too wrote the dialogue for her picture.

The next opportunity to practice the skill came in a writing assignment which was suggested during the "Right to Write" workshop given by NCTE at Cherry Hill, New Jersey in 1977. I made up a Progress Report (instead of a report card) for a fictional character, Marvin Termite, which contained poor grades and comments, and I instructed the children to write the conversation between Marvin and his mother about his progress report. These were read, enjoyed, and discussed by and with the children. Those who still needed more practice were asked to write the conversation between Marvin's mother and teacher, as well as the conversation between Marvin's mother and father about the report. I did not have children read each other's work, but this could also be done to demonstrate the clarity or lack of it as a result of punctuation.

I hope that after the completion of this series of structured exercises, the children's writing will contain more examples of dialogue correctly paragraphed and punctuated. Evaluation of the efficiency of the instruction will be made by the presence and use of punctuation marks in the children's free writing. Should some children still demonstrate the need for further instruction, additional exercises could be designed. Perhaps some selections of conversation from their reading material could be put on tape, and children who require practice could punctuate the selection and check it with the printed version. At all times, children were instructed to notice the use of the conventions in the printed material they were reading.

In designing these instructional strategies I tried to follow certain principles. First of all, there must be a great deal of writing in a free atmosphere so that the children can stretch themselves beyond the skills which they have already been taught. The children themselves must become aware of the need for instruction in a particular skill. The skill must be introduced to children who have the necessary knowledge on which to build the new skill, rather than to the entire class at one time. Practice exercises should be appealing, utilize differing approaches, and allow for variety of interpretation. Follow-up work for students who require it should be designed, and those who have mastered the skill should be encouraged to use the new or perfected skill in their own writing. Although our major concern remains with the expression of ideas, we also promote fluency when we equip children with the conventions of written composition with which to express themselves clearly and precisely.

Let's Hear It for the Preposition!

Mildred D. Berkowitz, Dartmouth Middle School,
New Bedford, Massachusetts

"Over the river
And through the woods,
To Grandmother's house
We go."

"Okay," says the teacher (of language arts) brightly, "what's the subject (of the sentence)?"

(In the class), ten hands shoot up positively, four hands flutter undecidedly, the other sixteen do not have an opinion when polled.

"David?" queries the teacher (in breathless anticipation).

"River," flashes David (with understandable self-satisfaction).

"Can anyone improve (on David's answer)?" asks this same educational paragon (in the approved style)(of Haim Ginott).

"Over!" shouts one (of our more creative grammar students), hardly waiting (for the teacher's nod)(in his eagerness)(for approbation).

The final scene (of this recurrent and all-too-familiar bitter classroom tragedy) is written when (at the urging)(of the teacher) (for still more "improvement"), one student offers "the" (as the subject).

This tragic vignette is not so far-fetched considering that textbook writers and teachers of English consistently overlook the relative importance of the humble preposition in our language. We treat it like a poor relation. It is either given a grudging page or two in the textbooks or, where its functional usefulness receives proper acknowledgement, it is accorded low priority in the hierarchy of what is to be taught. Granted, there are not too many of us leaping out of bathtubs and running down the street shouting, "Eureka!" Still, in our contemplation of the knotty problem of sequence for teaching of parts of speech (if we decide that grammer should be taught at all), some of us might have discovered that we are missing not only the bathtub, but the whole boat, by not teaching the preposition early and often.

Fairly sound reasons can be offered for the teaching of the noun and the verb as a first priority. We know that English is a language of word order; a subject-predicate language; a noun-verb language. Current textbooks and teaching techniques assume that we agree with the linguists that, minimally, there are four basic sentence patterns: N–V (noun-verb); N–V–N (noun-verb-noun); N–LV–N (noun-linking verb-noun); and N–LV–Adj (noun–linking verb–adjective). So if we want to get "back to basics," we had jolly well better know a noun and a verb when we see one."

Yet even with all the teaching techniques at hand, even with all the information on form, function, markers, patterning, and (excuse the expression) diagramming, why is it students still cannot identify the simple subject and the main verb in a sentence? Perhaps it is because we tend to ignore the fact that most English sentences consist of a series of phrases strung together. If the "bare bones" of the skeleton is the sentence pattern, then the meat on the bones is the ubiquitous preposition and the company it keeps, the elements of the prepositional phrase.

As a matter of purity, the preposition is not a preposition at all unless it is a part of a prepositional phrase—and at the very beginning of the phrase, at that. In a language riddled with exceptions, here is one of the steadfast verities which can be taught with confidence: A prepositional phrase *always* begins with a preposition and ends with a noun or noun substitute. For the transitional or structural linguists, it can be represented as (Prep + [Det or Adj] + N).

From a random choice of language arts textbooks and workbooks at the elementary, junior high, and senior high school levels, we can find a sentence to illustrate the work to be performed by underlining the simple subject once and the main verb twice:

1. The <u>mayor</u> of the city <u>ordered</u> the parade for Saturday.

Or, a sentence like this to show how to label sentence patterns:

2. The vicious tiger lurked in the deep jungle.

Every working classroom teacher will immediately see the pitfalls. It would be safe to wager that in the first instance, the teacher could find the students underlining any two words in the sentence, and in the second example, the N–V–N pattern would be chosen incorrectly more often than not. Now, in Example 1, if the words *of the city* and *for Saturday* are isolated by parentheses immediately, what is left to work with is: *The mayor ordered the parade.* There is much less chance for error and the meaning and intent show up cleanly and clearly. Again, in Example 2, if the words *in the deep jungle* are set apart with parentheses first, to look like this: *The vicious tiger lurked (in the deep jungle)*, it would be difficult to make an error in identifying the sentence pattern with what is left to label.

We err, it would seem, when we do not consider the prepositional phrase as a functioning *unit* at all times. As soon as we allow the phrase to be presented in a fluid, or unstable state, we are creating an artificial representation of the structure of our language. Additionally, we do violence to the form of the whole by breaking it into its parts before its total form and function can be clearly understood and absorbed.

In several current workbooks, the preposition is presented as a noun marker, which, of course, it is. But how much more efficiently it would perform this task if it were first set apart as a prepositional phrase unit. The final noun in the phrase would not so easily be mistaken, and the margin for error would decrease. Under a heading like, "Identifying Nouns by Their Signals," and with instructions to "draw a straight line under the determiners, a wavy line under the prepositions, then circle all the nouns," a typical passage such as this appears in a workbook:

In a few (minutes) the (dog) emerged from the (house) and sat down near the (horse) The old (horse) licked the black (hound) with his rough (tongue) and was affectionately pawed on the (nose) in (return.)

If, instead of dissolving each prepositional phrase into the body of the text, it is isolated as a unit and as a first task preceding the other instructions, it would appear that the nouns and their determiner markers would be much more easily and surely identified. It would look like this:

(In a few (minutes)) the (dog) emerged (from the (house)) and sat down (near the (horse)) The old (horse) licked the black (hound) (with his rough (tongue)) and was affectionately pawed (on the (nose)) (in (return))

Even the newer texts with transformational grammar orientation succumb to the trap. The prepositional phrase is presented in this fashion in the branching diagrams:

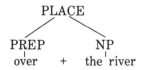

The visual representation again breaks the unit of the phrase into its deepest structure before its surface structure can be understood as a whole.

Recognized for all of its virtues, the preposition, that handy little speech part, as it combines with other words to form a prepositional phrase, is central to our language. The preposition offers direction in analyzing the structure of English sentences, adds variety and spice to the syntax in its role as phrase modifier and sentence expander, and is largely responsible for the lilt and rhythm which distinguishes the intonation of the English language from other languages. So ubiquitous are the prepositional phrases in our sentences, we are often not consciously aware of them, but like the poor relations spoken of earlier, they are always with us.

Periods Are Basic:
A Strategy for Eliminating
Comma Faults and Run-On
Sentences

Betty Bamberg, University of Southern California

In an effort to help students completely eradicate run-ons and comma faults, I have devised an instructional strategy which relies upon students' intuitive knowledge of grammar—competence in the Chomskyan sense—rather than upon their knowledge of formal grammar. I am convinced that students are better able to avoid run-on sentences and comma faults if they see that punctuation marks are related to the basic structure of language. This approach doesn't really teach a student anything new; instead it increases awareness of the intonation signals used in speech, shows the relationship between these signals and certain punctuation marks, and helps transfer this information to the student's own writing. That students can make use of intonation signals to punctuate their writing is hardly a new or original idea. However, instruction in learning to use one's intuitive knowledge of intonation appears to be neither systematic nor widespread. Those students who do use intonation signals to punctuate their writing seem to have learned this strategy on their own. Others can profit from some kind of assistance in learning to transfer their knowledge of intonation patterns to punctuate their writing. For these students, the lab has developed a five-stage procedure. The laboratory situation lends itself to individual work, using a tape recorder and a set of earphones. However, this strategy can easily be adapted for use with either a small group or an entire class.

During the first three stages, the student listens to recorded readings of a controlled text. She is asked to punctuate the text, and is gradually led to rely exclusively on intonation signals to place periods and commas. In the final two stages, the student examines her own punctuation, first by listening to a recorded version of her writing and checking the punctuation marks used, then by checking as she reads her writing aloud. Correct answers follow each segment of Stages 1-3, so a student can determine whether she is ready to move to the next stage or whether she should ask for a back-up tape which provides additional practice. In Stages 4 and 5, a writing tutor checks the student's work to ensure that all run-ons and comma faults have been eliminated. The following outline describes each stage and illustrates the materials used at each level.

Stage I

The intonation patterns associated with the period and comma are explained to the student. She is shown the notations which will be used in the text to symbolize the pauses (junctures) and changes in pitch. The fade-fall pitch and terminal pause, which is punctuated in writing by a period, is shown as ⌄ , while the slightly raised or level pitch followed by a briefer pause (punctuated by a comma) is shown as ↗, or →. Then the student listens to several paragraphs, simultaneously reading a text which contains both punctuation marks and linguistic symbols illustrating the pitch and juncture patterns.

> My profession as a journalist has often allowed me to attend trials.⌄ The Brentwood murder was,↗ however,↗ one of the most curious affairs that I had ever experienced in my life.⌄ Apparently,↗ it was a clear case,→ open and shut with no doubt about it.*⌄

Once the student is able to hear the differences in intonation patterns between the comma and the period, she moves to the second stage.

Stage II

The student continues to listen to a tape and to read an accompanying text. However, commas and periods have been removed, with a cue (an underline) indicating each place where one is needed.

> The accused was a short and heavily-built man___ there in the dock with two policemen standing guard___ he looked like a wild animal with terrible strength___ his eyes were dark and fierce.

The student must put either a period or a comma where each

---

*John D. Edwards, "A Clear Case," *Multi-Read* (Chicago: SRA, 1973).

underline appears, basing her choice on the intonation signal she hears. When she has no difficulty punctuating a cued paragraph correctly, she is ready to move to the third stage, punctuating a text with no visual cues.

Stage III

At this level, the student must rely entirely on intonational signals. As she listens to the tape recording, she punctuates a text like the following:

> He was the sort of character you didn't forget if you had seen him only once the counsel for the prosecution dressed in his black robes had several witnesses who remembered seeing Jones coming out of the red house a little after two o'clock in the morning.

Stages IV and V

The student is now ready to apply this increased awareness of intonation signals to her own writing. Good oral readers encounter little difficulty with this task, but poor readers frequently need help in reading with the rhythms, emphases, and phrasing of their everyday speech. Students who have difficulty reading aloud are coached by writing tutors who instruct them to preread their work silently before attempting to read it orally and to work with one paragraph units. In Stage IV the student records her writing, then replays the tape to check the punctuation, particularly listening for places where the intonation signals indicate that a period should be used. Once she can identify run-ons or comma faults in this recorded version, she moves to Stage V, where she reads her essay aloud and checks the punctuation without the assistance of a recorder.

This technique does not help students learn the correct placement of all punctuation marks, but it has been very successful in teaching them to use periods correctly, thereby eliminating comma faults and run-on sentences. Encouraging students to read their writing aloud as a regular step in the final editing of an essay has several other desirable outcomes as well. As they read, students frequently discover other errors (especially omitted words or word endings and awkward or unclear phrasing) which they correct at the same time they are checking their punctuation. Equally important, the student gains a sense of confidence about her knowledge of language and her ability to use that knowledge to master a basic skill.

Alternatives to Tradition in Teaching Spelling

Anne Ruggles Gere, University of Washington, Seattle

Spelling ranks high and often takes first place on lists of basic skills. Misspelled words are relatively easy to spot; any layperson with a modicum of education can locate orthographic errors. Although English has some variant spellings (traveled, travelled), orthography is rarely controversial or subject to individual interpretation as are many issues of usage. It is not surprising, then, that business people, legislators, the media, and the general public are united on the primacy of correct spelling in "basic education."

Uniformity of opinion on the importance of spelling is matched by uniformity in teaching it. Generations of students throughout the land have been assigned weekly word lists and quizzed on Fridays. Yet we cannot claim that this method has produced a nation of accurate spellers. And student testimony reveals the negative attitudes we have fostered; junior high students look forward to high school "because we won't have any more spelling tests." True, but the red "sp" will serve as replacement. I propose alternatives to weekly word lists and red marks.

Individualized word lists are much more effective than arbitrary selections. Students can create their own lists from words they have to look up in the dictionary, words misspelled in their written work, words suggested by/traded with friends, and unfamiliar words discussed by the teacher. Teachers can answer the reflexive "how do you spell..." with appropriate letters and an admonition to add the word to the individualized list. Alphabetical divisions in a notebook form a mini-dictionary where students' personal word lists are kept; as an additional challenge students can be asked to put a check beside a word each time they need to look it up. Weekly assessment of progress in spelling can likewise be individualized. Each student submits ten words from his or her personal list and is quizzed on them by the teacher, an aide, or another student. Success with a word on two or three tests entitles the student to retire the word from the active list.

In the time which would be spent introducing weekly word lists, conducting pretests, or circling "alot" on student papers, the teacher can offer strategies for improving spelling. Classroom games can ensure that students become active users of dictionaries. For example, timed contests to find correct spellings of difficult words provide fun and opportunities for learning with, not about, a dictionary. Difficult or challenging words will, of course, vary with class ability, but general categories of misspellings include: vowels in unaccented syllables (discribe–describe, instramental–instrumental, prevelent–prevalent, relevence–relevance, poisen–poison); unnecessary letters (assett–asset, curiousity–curiosity, deriogatory–derogatory, symbollic–symbolic, barbarious–barbarous, arguement–argument, truely–truly); omitted letters (minature–miniature, involvment–involvement, embarass–embarrass, supressed–suppressed, impetous–impetuous); confusion of two words (its–it's, loose–lose, too–to, course–coarse, they're–their, boarder–border, desert–dessert, whether–weather); transposed letters (sieze–seize, prespiration–perspiration, wierd–weird); and substituted letters (surprize–surprise, recognise–recognize, inconciderate–inconsiderate). Teachers can select words of appropriate difficulty, divide the class into teams of 2–5, distribute dictionaries to everyone or every team, read the words in context and challenge teams to use dictionaries to find correct spellings. Declare as winner the first team to submit a list with all words spelled correctly. Hearing words in context and using the dictionary as a resource approximates the actual spelling tasks students perform as they write—they "hear" a word they wish to use and then try to spell it.

The utility of commonly taught spelling "rules" is limited. The most widely known, I *before* E *except after* C *or when sounded as* [E] *as in neighbor and weigh*, can be helpful only to students who are relatively accurate spellers. In order to apply the rule one must know that the word to be spelled involves the sound [i] spelled either *IE* or *EI*; [i] is spelled *IE* in only 2.2% of all English words and *EI* in less than one percent of its occurrences in English. One would need to know that the sound before the [i] in question is spelled *C* not *S*; *S* is the more common representation for [s]. And one would need to know that the word in question was not one of the exceptions to the rule such as *neither* and *seize*.

An alternative to teaching spelling "rules" is to teach brief lessons on phoneme-grapheme correspondences, to show students that English lacks one sound to one letter correspondence. The sound [k], for example, is produced by *C* (cattle), *K* (kettle), and *CK* (jack). The letter *S*, on the other hand, can be pronounced [ž] (decision), [z] (busy), and [s] (sue). English vowels are particularly difficult for spellers because one symbol produces a variety of sounds. For example, for 69.49% of occurrences of the sound [a] in English, the sound is spelled *O*. The work of Paul R. Hanna, Jean S. Hanna, Richard E. Hodges, and Edwin H. Rudorf, *Phoneme-Grapheme Correspondences as Cues to Spelling Improvement* (Washington D.C.: U.S. Department of Health, Education and Welfare, 1966. OE 32008) offers extensive information on sound-symbol relationships and provides materials for many brief lessons on spelling.

Another alternative to teaching spelling "rules" is to make students aware of morpheme consistency in English. For example, the past tense morpheme is always spelled *-ED* whether it is pronounced [t] (hoped), [d] (beamed), or [əd] (wanted). The morpheme *bomb* remains consistent when it appears in the longer *bombard*; *photo* appears consistently in *photography* and *photographic*. Noam Chomsky and Morris Halle's *The Sound Pattern of English* (New York: Harper and Row, 1968) offers many examples of morpheme consistency and attempts to state the rules which determine the correspondence between underlying phonological form and spelling. Both grapheme-phoneme correspondences and morpheme consistency can be taught in frequent short interactive sessions where class attention is focused on a particular issue—how many ways can we represent the sound [f]—and underlying principles can be deduced.

Ability to divide words into syllables can be a powerful tool in improving spelling because many orthographic errors result from transcribing the blurred forms of spoken English. Students who can separate words into component parts are more likely to notice the omitted syllable in clercal (clerical) or surban (suburban). In *Spelling: Structures and Strategies* (Boston: Houghton Mifflin, 1971), authors Paul R. Hanna, Richard Hodges, and Jean S. Hanna suggest that students can induce principles of syllabication by examining word lists that illustrate the most useful principles of syllabication. Their recommendations (p. 229) provide ready-made lessons.

Teaching spelling in secondary school does not end in the classroom, however. The current national preoccupation with standardized tests has the potential to undermine even the most effective spelling instruction. In 1977 nearly half the state legislatures in the United States considered bills mandating standardized tests for various grade levels. We know that spelling is encoding, representing sounds in graphic form, yet the spelling tests on commonly used standardized tests are decoding, reading tasks where students indicate whether or not words are spelled correctly. The majority of these "spelling" sections have a large number of words misspelled, often more than 70%. Thus, students are having visual encounters with many misspelled words and are likely to store this inaccurate orthography.

Effective teaching of spelling involves, then, activity outside the classroom as well as within it. Within the classroom we can individualize spelling instruction so that it has a direct relation to other aspects of students' work with language and so that students become more responsible for their own learning rather than depending upon external stimuli. Beyond the classroom we can inform the public of the difference between encoding and decoding, show the weaknesses of spelling sections on most standardized tests and insist that state-mandated tests offer true measures of orthography. When we do both we will be teaching spelling—really.

The Big Five: Individualizing Improvement in Spelling

Muriel Harris, Purdue University

For college freshmen who find that they must work on spelling, the few pages in the textbook are inadequate, a programmed spelling book is too lengthy, and weekly tests derived either from lists of commonly misspelled words or from the mistakes in other students' papers give no insight into their own spelling habits. What students about to approach the task of studying spelling really need is some motivation to expend their time and effort on the rather pedestrian business of learning where to put the *ie*'s, double *l*'s, and elusive syllables. Students also need to become aware of their own habitual errors and not everyone else's, and finally, they need to discriminate between the everyday work-horse words that they must often have at their fingertips and the more difficult or less frequently used words for which they need dictionary skills. The classroom strategy that I have used for this isn't infallible, but the results are usually quite good because it does allow spelling work to become individualized, even in the classroom.

What is needed, before beginning our work, is a fairly lengthy sample of the students' spelling habits. Since, in my classes, the students immerse themselves for the first few weeks in free writing, journal writing, structured essay writing, etc., we have, by the third or fourth week of the semester, a rather representative sample of each student's writing. The misspellings in this writing are considered the raw data which we will analyze. To help the students collect this data, I indicate which words were misspelled on all papers written during the first few weeks, and I ask only that the students list somewhere their misspelled words exactly as they have originally written them and then put the correct spelling next to their version of the word. I don't expect much improvement from this technique, and there is usually only a minimal gain.

Before I make any formal announcement that we will do some intensive work on spelling, I bring to class several short letters to the editor from the student newspaper, a local newspaper, or a national news magazine. In several, but not all of those letters, I misspell some of the more common words on the copies given to the students. As we discuss the points these writers are trying to make and compare the degree to which they adequately support their arguments, our attention begins to focus on the writers themselves. As we weigh our perceptions of these writers, members of the class usually begin to look askance at the writers whose letters have the misspellings. Sometimes a student will snicker that someone who misspells "actually" is hardly likely to be a deep thinker; at other times the cause of the disparaging comments are not pinned down quite so overtly. However, we normally wind up less impressed with those writers who have seemingly misspelled many words.

That such results can be expected was recently confirmed in a study done at Arizona State University, in which freshmen were asked to rate prose under several conditions (with all words correctly spelled, with every ninth word misspelled, and with all content words misspelled). In this study, the student raters considered the writers of the misspelled versions as "being less educated, less neat, less intelligent and more masculine than the good spellers." I could cite this study to my class (and perhaps discuss why women are considered to be better spellers than men), but I believe that it is more effective for students to become aware of their own reactions toward poor spelling, and that is, simply, that we are more likely (either consciously or unconsciously) to consider a poor speller as more careless or less intelligent than an accurate speller. And there are times when such an attitude toward our misspellings can cost us dearly, as, for example, when a prospective employer reads a job application.

Having reached a consensus that some attention to spelling is worthwhile, we are ready to proceed. What we do is intended to result in a more careful analysis by each student of some of the ways in which he or she tends to be led astray by certain vowels, consonants, and syllables in the more commonly used words. I begin by listing five categories likely to cause the writer problems with frequently used words (the category names having been suggested by students):

1. *Homophone Hang-ups.* In this category are all those troublesome sound-alikes that can plague us, e.g.,

their/there/they're
your/you're
then/than
its/it's
too/to/two
here/hear
past/passed

While I try to explain the different meanings of each word, the emphasis of the discussion is that it is easy to confuse similar-sounding words.

2. *Probe Your Pronunciation.* In this category are those words which can be misspelled because the writer is trying to reproduce his own elided or inaccurate pronunciation of a word. This produces misspellings such as "probley," "preform" (for "perform"), "represenative," "promply," "govment," "practicly," etc. The students are not asked to change their speaking habits, only to become aware that the written form for some common words is different from the spoken word and that speech cues cannot be relied on for the spelling of such words.

3. *To Double or Not to Double the Consonant.* The purpose of this very useful category is to point out that we don't usually double a consonant unless:

 a. The "-ly" suffix is added to a word which already has a final "l." This covers the common misspellings such as "realy," "mentaly," "actualy," "finaly," etc.

 b. A suffix beginning with a vowel ("-ing" or "-ed") is being added to a single-syllable word with one short vowel and then a consonant or to a word with the accent on the last syllable. This group covers frequently written errors such as "begining," "runing," "writting," "developped," "sweatted," etc. Thus, unless there is a good reason to double the consonant, such as with a prefix (e.g., "interrupt," "dissolve," "appoint," etc.), don't. Students can then include in this category misspellings such as "bussiness," "immage," or "errase."

4. *Getting to the Root of the Problem.* When students write forms such as "discription," "humerous," or "unexeptional," they can sometimes correctly spell the root or base words but lose sight of the known base as the additions are included.

5. *Guess the Schwa (ə).* Once students become aware of how often the schwa sound occurs and why it offers no clue to the

vowel needed, they can see the difficulties which result in misspellings such as "grammer," "independance," "attendence," "seperate," and "benifit."

Once we have discussed these five categories and the class is fairly familiar with what should be included in each, the students are ready to begin analyzing their own particular spelling difficulties. The class is divided into small groups consisting of no more than four or five students. The initial task of each student is to look at his or her list of misspellings and then place under each of our categories those misspellings which are appropriate to the category. Members of the groups are encouraged to help each other, and I roam around the room acting as a consultant. Those students who have no misspellings or only a very few are asked to assist me as additional roving consultants. As the students look at their misspellings, discuss them, analyze them, and try to fit as many as possible under each heading, they very often find errors which cannot be classified under the categories I have set up. If these words are the less often used or more difficult ones, they are labeled "See Dictionary." For other words that defy classification, we resort to the heading "Other" because, as I warn the class, we are not after all their misspellings, only a reasonable chunk of them. Occasionally, a student can create a new category, but none have yet matured into a generally applicable category.

One final step remains. When students have classified as many of their spelling errors as they can, they are ready to draw up their own profiles by rank ordering the categories; category #1 is the group with the most entries, and so on. When the students are finished, they not only have a working knowledge of some ways in which they are likely to misspell commonly used words, they also have a profile of which groups most frequently cause them problems. When this process is complete, students are better able to define and identify their own spelling weaknesses, and simultaneously evolve better methods of attacking the spelling of a word.

The Best of Two Worlds

Mary E. Commers, Lincoln Southeast High School, Lincoln, Nebraska

"Be not the first by whom the new is tried,
Nor yet the last to put the old aside."

These lines of Alexander Pope guided some successful action research in both my sophomore and senior English classes, inspired by an NCTE convention where I had heard Frank O'Hare explain and illustrate the principles of sentence combining and where I had purchased a copy of William Strong's book, *Sentence Combining*. In my action research, the principles of sentence combining constituted the "new," and a review of prepositional phrases, verbal phrases, nominative absolutes, appositives, subordinate clauses, and parallel structures, such as items in series, constituted the "old."

In my sophomore class, I used the following two groups of sentences to introduce some biographical facts on both William Shakespeare and Julius Caesar before our study of Shakespeare's drama. Students rewrote the two groups of sentences into two coherent sentences using, if possible, a variety of sentence structures.

Shakespeare was born at Stratford-on-Avon.
Shakespeare was a dramatist.
He was an English dramatist.
He was a great dramatist.
He was born in the year 1564.
He was born during the reign of Queen Elizabeth.

Julius Caesar was a Roman statesman.
He was a general.
He was an excellent politician.
He was an outstanding statesman.
He was a skillful writer.
He was forceful in oratory.

108

He is a controversial figure in history.
Some consider him a brilliant ruler.
Others think him a power-hungry dictator.

In introducing the modern prose style of Jonathan Swift's *Gulliver's Travels*, I gave my seniors copies of the following groups of sentences and directed them to combine each group into a logical sentence. Later I provided the page numbers of the *Gulliver's Travels* text and asked students to compare their revised sentences with those of Swift.

About three years ago Mr. Gulliver, growing weary of the concourse of curious people coming to him at his house in Redriff, made a small purchase of land, with a convenient house, near Newark in Nottinghamshire, his native country.

Mr. Gulliver made a small purchase of land.
The purchase was made about three years ago.
Mr. Gulliver had grown weary of the concourse of curious people.
The curious people came to him at his house in Redriff.
The land had a convenient house.
It was located near Newark in Nottinghamshire.
Nottinghamshire was his native country.

When I came back, I resolved to settle in London, to which Mr. Bates, my master, encouraged me, and by him I was recommended to several patients.

I came back.
I resolved to settle in London.
My master encouraged me to settle in London.
My master was Mr. Bates.
Mr. Bates recommended me to several patients.

After three years' expectation that things would mend, I accepted an advantageous offer from Captain William Prichard, master of the *Antelope*, who was making a voyage to the South Seas.

For three years I had expectations.
My expectations were that things would mend.
I accepted an advantageous offer from Captain William Prichard.
William Prichard was master of the *Antelope*.
He was making a voyage to the South Seas.

On the fifth of November which was the beginning of summer in those parts, the weather being very hazy, the seaman spied a rock, within half a cable's length of the ship.

It was the fifth of November.
The fifth of November was the beginning of summer in those parts.
The weather was hazy.

The seaman spied a rock.
The rock was within half a cable's length of the ship.

The sempstresses took my measure as I lay on the ground, one standing at my neck, and another at my midleg, with a strong cord extended that each held by the end, while the third measured the length of the cord with a rule of an inch long.

The semptresses took my measure.
They took my measure as I lay on the ground.
One stood at my neck.
Another stood at my midleg.
They extended a strong cord.
Each sempstress held the cord by the end.
A third sempstress measured the length of the cord.
They measured with a rule of an inch long.

His features are strong and masculine, with an Austrian lip and arched nose, his complexion olive, his countenance erect, his body and limbs well proportioned, all his motions graceful, and his deportment majestic.

His features are strong.
His features are masculine.
He has an Austrian lip and arched nose.
His complexion is olive.
His countenance is erect.
His body and limbs are well proportioned.
His motions are graceful.
His deportment is majestic.

In the action research conducted with my sophomore and senior classes, my students profited from the best of two worlds: the "old" with the review of basic sentence structures, and the "new" with the sentence-combining theories of Mr. O'Hare and Mr. Strong. Sentence-combining exercises lend themselves well to many works of literature; the students have practice in improving their own style while studying that of a master, and the teacher is ingeniously approaching a study of basics in sentence structure. Truly the teacher can combine Pope's "new" and "old."

Sentence Modeling to Develop Syntactic Fluency

Raymond J. Rodrigues, University of Utah, Salt Lake City

Sentence modeling is a technique to develop students' abilities to manipulate syntax structures according to the students' purposes, their intended audiences, and the occasions for writing. For those who demand a return to basics, it is a technique which rhetoric classes employed long before Reed and Kellogg dissected the sentence and left it pinned down in the tray of prescriptivism.

The rationale for sentence modeling is based upon several related observations. First, a number of established authors have maintained that, in their apprentice years, they tried copying the styles of their favorite authors. Second, after observing the natural language development of children, linguists concluded that young children model their language production upon adult speech. For some children, the process is overt; they practice new syntax patterns over and over in private. And third, many writing teachers argue that they can determine which of their students read widely by selecting those students who write best. These students have somehow subconsciously absorbed models of good writing and are able to select from those models when they themselves are writing. The common denominator in all these instances appears to be the modeling process, whether consciously performed or not.

Certain syntax structures are noticeably absent in less mature writers. In some instances, entire classes may never employ a particuarly syntax structure in their writing. As a process, sentence modeling forces students to use syntax structures they may occasionally use in speaking, but seldom, if ever, in writing. It is a technique which applies at any grade level. If, for example, an elementary teacher wants students to use a structure as simple as three adjectives in a series, the teacher can create sentences to be modeled:

"The dog was big, fat, and brown."
"The big, fat, brown dog is mine."

111

Or the teacher can find examples in student readers, examples which are often surprisingly mature:

> "Although Jim didn't see him, an old white male wolf was lying on the shadowy ledge."
>
> William S. Briscoe

If students need help with a particular syntax structure, the teacher can offer a model sentence and ask students for original sentences based on that model. For example, if a junior high school class does not employ nouns in series modified by parallel prepositional phrases, the teacher could require that the following sentence be modeled:

> "I am an American by birth, a Nazi by reputation, and a nationless person by inclination."
>
> Kurt Vonnegut, Jr.

Based upon that, a student might write:

> "He was a teacher at school, a father at home, and a dismal failure at both."

Less mature writers seldom employ prepositional phrases or subordinate clauses at the beginnings of their sentences. In that case, the teacher would want to select sentences which do, such as:

> "In the pockets under the red earth banks, where the wind was cut off, the spring sun was hot as summer, and the air was full of a hot, melting pine smell."
>
> Walter Van Tilburg Clark

Note, however, that maturity in syntactic flexibility does not imply that sentences must be long and convoluted. So, more capable students could model short but mature structures:

> "The only touch of green we could see was far away, beyond the tracks, over where the white folks lived."
>
> Richard Wright

The building of prepositional phrase upon prepositional phrase is a delight in the hands of such a capable writer.

For variety, students need ability in creating the occasional long sentence:

> "Leaving the car near the little church within its low mud wall, they walked into the corona of filth and acrid odor of urine and ordure that edged the pueblo, past the lanes opening between rows of squat, flat-topped houses."
>
> Frank Waters

The sentences can be selected from the literature the students are reading or from actual productions of student writing.

So that students are not inundated with sentence modeling exercises, potentially diminishing the technique's effectiveness, a teacher can elect to have students model only one good sentence each week. Then, to ensure that students employ the model, the teacher can require that a sentence modeled upon the original be included somewhere in a writing assignment for the week. It will be an easy matter for the teacher to identify the modeled sentence.

A variation upon this technique is to have students fill in the blanks in sentence models:

"If you're not part of the solution, you're part of the problem."
Eldridge Cleaver

The students then complete the following:

If you're not _____, you're _____.

By projecting the variations with an overhead projector, the teacher may lead the class in discussing the syntactic accuracy of the student sentences, the effectiveness of the new inventions, and the importance or impact of what each student has written, thus rewarding students not only for their ability to model syntax structures, but also for developing meaningful ideas. Particularly effective sentences produced by students, sentences which move students emotionally and intellectually, may become the foundations for future writing assignments. Thus, what began as a relatively simple modeling assignment will have expanded to encompass the major thinking, speaking, and writing efforts of the class.

As a class masters the sentence modeling technique, the teacher can advance to whole paragraph modeling. Paragraph modeling is a more difficult task, but students will soon realize that paragraph syntax must correlate with the subject or purpose of the paragraph; not all paragraph patterns are appropriate for all subjects. Students may have to experiment with different subjects before finding one which lends itself to the exact structures employed in the model paragraph. A descriptive passage filled with embedded adjectival phrases may not suit an argumentative purpose. But a paragraph such as the one with which Poe opens his "Fall of the House of Usher" may well serve as a model for a student to describe her first impressions of school or his first day at high school football practice.

The teaching techniques essentially remain the same for paragraph modeling as for sentence modeling. Students might have to begin by substituting single words, rather than by trying to model the entire paragraph from first word to last period. From replacing single words, they might move to substituting phrases and then entire clauses. Moreover, in modeling entire paragraphs, students learn to perceive the interrelation of syntax structures *between sentences*. Transitions and pronoun references take on new meaning. Generalities clearly must be related to specifics. The unity of the paragraph must be maintained. And the syntax thereby supports the meaning, rather than being something taught in isolation from linguistic creativity.

Modeling of sentences and paragraphs is not an artificial technique; it is natural to the language learning process. It also justifies our teaching literature when critics are calling for a return to grammar and writing exercises. Sentence modeling is a reflection of the natural processes of language development, is relatively painless in its application, is adjustable to the linguistic abilities of students at all levels of syntactic fluency, and, happily, does not require students to identify one syntax structure by name.

5 About Teaching Listening, Creative Thinking, and Discussion

One of the challenges in teaching English is that it encompasses such a wide variety of subjects and skills. Here, one teacher offers an exercise designed to teach elementary students how to listen—really listen. Another reminds us that although *con*vergent thinking deserves an important place in the secondary curriculum, we must also encourage *di*vergent thinking; the creative thinking process is the basis for writing, yet it is so often neglected. Finally, students are exposed to a three-ring discussion procedure which lets them discover what works in a discussion situation, and how to focus on specifics in a written evaluation.

Listening Skill: The Basic Basic

John D. Stammer, University of Toledo, Ohio

Listening is a skill requiring a *clear* message and a *receptive* listener. Neither of these factors can be taken for granted in a classroom. It may seem that a good deal of what the teacher has to say is distorted or misinterpreted by children, but when students fail to follow a teacher's directions accurately, the teacher's assumption that the directions are *mis*interpreted may not be correct. What more likely has occurred is that the children have indeed *interpreted* the message, rather than followed it literally. These children need activities which focus on processing and responding to a message requiring literal or factual comprehension.

To help children improve their skills in following directions and literal listening, the process of assimilating directions and then constructing a map has a high degree of application at almost any level of elementary school. To accomplish this task children need only a sheet of paper and a pen, pencil, or crayon. They listen to directions and construct a map.

It is the responsibility of the teacher to establish the best listening environment possible, but directions for the task completion may vary. Since this task should be a nonthreatening one, teachers may prefer not to warn children about doing only what they are explicitly told to do. Omitting such a warning will increase the probability of error, and provide an opportunity to demonstrate graphically to the children points where listening was careless.

Primary Direction Set

This set is designed for early first-grade children but can be modified and adapted as the children become more facile in their skill.

1. Draw a line across the middle of your paper.
2. There is a line through the middle of the paper from top to bottom also.
3. There is an 'X' near the top of the paper.
4. Put the word YES near the bottom right corner of the paper.
5. Draw a square in the lower left corner of the paper.
6. Put a circle in the middle of the paper.
7. There is a small triangle in the circle.

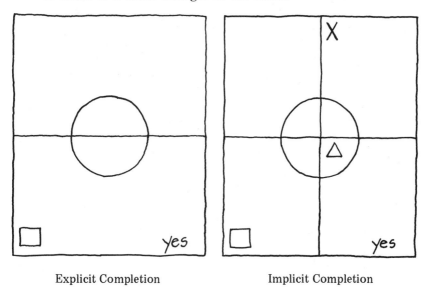

Explicit Completion   Implicit Completion

Fig. 1. Implicit and explicit task completion for primary grade students.

Figure 1 indicates there may be a discrepancy between the teacher's directions and those lines the children have drawn. Directions two, three, and seven do *not* ask the children to include (draw..., place..., put...) them on the map. It seems predictable that the task *will be interpreted* and therefore will be wrong. The errors will be apparent to the children after discussion and they will have a better understanding of the need to listen to and follow directions carefully. Future exercises can provide opportunities for the children to function in a thinking mode and permit correct completion. The imaginative teacher can construct almost infinite direction sets, simplifying or sophisticating them as required.

Intermediate Direction Set

At the intermediate level children may or may not be familiar with compass points. Figure 2 includes such points, and assumes about a third grade level of ability. As with the primary activity, directions may vary but the listening mode needs to be established prior to giving the direction set.

1. Main St. runs east-west through the center of town. Put it on your map and label it.
2. Center St. runs north-south through the center of town. Put it on your map.
3. A railroad runs north-south along the eastern edge of town. Put it on your map.
4. Jones High School is on the southwest corner of town. Put it on your map.
5. South St. runs parallel to Main St., and just north of the school from the edge of town to Center St.
6. City Hall is on the northeast corner of Main and Center.
7. School St. runs north-south along the east side of Jones High to Main St. Put it on your map and label it.
8. The train depot is on the northwest corner where Main St. and the tracks cross.

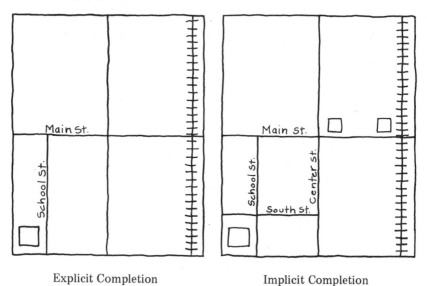

Explicit Completion   Implicit Completion

Fig. 2. Implicit and explicit task completion for intermediate grade students.

In viewing Figure 2, note the contrast between the implied or implicit directions and the explicit directions. Again, unless the student listens with care, assumptions are made and the map is incorrectly drawn. With this particular direction set, we do not label Center St., and we do not include South St., City Hall, or the train depot at all. As with the primary map task, the directions for this activity can be varied to meet the abilities and progress of the children.

The process of following directions through literal listening can be the foundation for increasingly complex listening encounters. The task for the children in completing the activities in this article is simplistic on the surface, but is an important aspect of the total process.

Helping Students
to Think Creatively

Jeffrey N. Golub, Kent Junior High School, Seattle,
Washington

Traditional classroom instruction at the secondary level is characterized by an emphasis upon the development of students' ability to engage in "convergent" thinking, and a consequent neglect of students' potential for creative thought and production. In the preface to their workbook, *New Directions in Creativity* (Harper & Row, 1973), Joseph S. Renzulli and Carolyn M. Callahan describe teachers' current practice of encouraging convergent thinking in the classroom:

> In most traditional teaching–learning situations, major emphasis is placed on locating or converging upon correct answers. Teachers raise questions and present problems with a predetermined response in mind, and student performance is usually evaluated in terms of the correctness of a particular answer and the speed and accuracy with which youngsters respond to verbal or written exercises. Thus the types of problems raised by the teacher or textbook and the system of rewards used to evaluate student progress cause most youngsters to develop a learning style that is oriented toward zeroing in on the "right" answer as quickly and as efficiently as possible. (p. 3)

The development of convergent thinking can be a valuable asset to students, and certainly deserves a place in the secondary curriculum. Mathematics and science courses, for instance, each have elaborate and precise methods for deriving a correct solution or answer to a variety of problems and in a variety of contexts. A problem arises, however, when English teachers, failing to see the uniqueness of their discipline, also attempt to structure their classroom content and activities to promote convergent thinking. A traditional approach to the teaching of grammar and an undue concentration upon the teaching and learning of literary terms are two examples of activities that require students to exercise their convergent thinking ability.

120

What is needed in secondary language arts classrooms is the development of students' potential for engaging in what is variously called "divergent," "lateral," or "creative" thinking. This process is a basic skill that permits students to generate many alternatives, and encourages the brainstorming of ideas. Renzulli and Callahan have identified four major components of creative thought:

1. *Fluency*—the ability to generate a ready flow of ideas, possibilities, consequences, and objects.
2. *Flexibility*—the ability to use many different approaches or strategies in solving a problem: the willingness to change direction and modify given information.
3. *Originality*—the ability to produce clever, unique, and unusual responses.
4. *Elaboration*—the ability to expand, develop, particularize, and embellish one's ideas, stories, and illustrations. (p. 4)

The development and utilization of one or more of these four processes involved in creative thinking are ideally suited to the language arts classroom. Generating topics for compositions, working with sentence-combining exercises, or discussing an issue, a film, a project in class, can all be facilitated by a unit devoted to the development of creative thinking. Students will begin to entertain and take advantage of ideas and possibilities that they would have previously rejected immediately as being impractical or silly. In addition, students will find themselves listening more intently to other students' responses, seeking to clarify rather than to evaluate contributions. A classroom climate of trust and acceptance is established as a result of a unit on creative thinking because of the de-emphasis of that potentially destructive element, evaluation.

Training students to brainstorm for ideas is a good way to promote fluency in generating alternatives, one of the components of creative thinking. Have the students arrange themselves into groups of 4-5 members, each group appointing a member to record the ideas generated. Announce that the following rules apply to the brainstorming sessions:

1. *The more ideas that are generated, the better.* Quantity is desired at this point, not quality.
2. *The wilder the ideas that are generated, the better.* This rule encourages students to consider outlandish possibilities which can later be modified into workable ideas.

3. *No evaluation of ideas is allowed.* This rule frees students from the fear of being criticized for their ideas and thus creates a climate conducive to the practice of divergent thinking.

Allow 3-5 minutes for the brainstorming of each topic. Mild intergroup competition may be introduced by listing on the blackboard the total number of ideas generated by each group after each session.

Suitable topics for initial brainstorming sessions might include:

1. List as many ways as you can think of to come to school in the morning.
   Examples: donkey, pogo-stick, rocket, parachute, etc.

2. Assuming you could change your size and shape, how could you come to school?
   Example: change into a drop of water and come to school in the drinking fountain, etc.
   (from *New Directions in Creativity*)

3. List possible names for cats.
   Examples: Chester, Sybil, Grice, Lissadel, Astrid, etc.

4. List possible names for elephants.
   Examples: Ormond, Bruce, Wilbur, Bendigo, Duff, Wendell Tubb, etc.
   (from *Language of Man*)

5. Make a list of things that come in or are associated with the number three.
   Examples: three blind mice, three sides of a triangle, triple-decker sandwich, etc.

6. Make a list of 100 ways to have fun with an alligator.
   Examples: put dry ice in his mouth and call the fire department, use his mouth as an ashtray, buy him a big red balloon at the fair, etc.
   (from *100 Ways to Have Fun with an Alligator...*)

7. List everything you can think of that is both soft and blue.
   Example: a fish that is dipped in blue paint, etc.
   (from *New Directions in Creativity*)

8. Think of as many uses as you can for the following items:
   a) old razor blades
   b) a door
   c) a button
   d) a newspaper

Other ideas can be found in the resources listed at the end of this article.

You should find that each successive brainstorming session yields a greater quantity of ideas than did the last one, as students gain confidence and skill in the practice of divergent thinking. After having conducted several initial brainstorming sessions, you can introduce more complex topics and begin to utilize the students' creative thinking skill as a tool to work on other language arts skills. For instance, consider this next series of topics and suggested follow-up activities.

9. You have just bought 65,000 old bricks for 2¢ each. The bricks were part of an old school building that has just been torn down to make room for a parking lot. You have the three summer months during which you plan to sell the 65,000 old bricks for 50¢ each, thereby making a profit of $31,200. Explain how you are going to manage to sell the bricks for 50¢ each. Assume that no one will buy the bricks in order to build a building.

10. Propose a solution to the traffic problem that involves ending all private ownership of automobiles. Propose that automobiles be supplied like shopping carts, left on streets for anyone to use. Explain this system in detail and work out possible problems.
(from *Creativity Kit*)

After the initial brainstorming of problems involved with the above idea, students might prepare an oral explanation and presentation of their "system" for the rest of the class.

11. Make a list of possible improvements for the common student desk. Then, pick *one* improvement from your list and convince the class that the improvement is (a) practical, (b) desirable, and (c) necessary.

12. a. Design a new eating implement that has as important a function as the knife, fork, and spoon.

b. Write a letter to a potential manufacturer of your new invention, convincing him or her that your idea is practical, necessary, and desirable, and persuading him or her to begin to make this product for sale to the world.

c. Design an ad for this eating implement.

Another aspect of creative thinking is the ability to see or to create connections between two or more apparently dissimilar objects, elements, or concepts. The ability to create similes and metaphors, for instance, is dependent upon the development and utilization of this skill. The following experiences, each of which allows students to "play with language," can serve as an exciting introduction or accompaniment to a unit on poetry and the devices of language manipulation employed by poets.

1. Charles Schultz, creator of the "Peanuts" cartoon strip, has written a book, *Happiness Is A Warm Puppy*, in which he gives concrete illustrations of the abstract quality "happiness" through "word-pictures." A few examples written on the blackboard will encourage students to begin creating their own word-pictures for their own abstract qualities.

   Examples:
   Loneliness is...an empty mailbox.
   Peace is...soft snow.
   Sadness is...your best friend moving away.
   (from *Write Now*)

   Encourage students to generate several word-pictures for each abstraction they choose, instead of settling for their first response only. A possible follow-up activity is to have students clip pictures from magazines that graphically illustrate an abstract concept, or to go out and photograph their own picture to illustrate a concept they have in mind.

2. Make a list of words that "sound" like what they mean (onomatopoeia). Examples: plump, clink, plop, tap, buzz. Make up a list of words that describe the sounds of each of the following (and feel free to create your own words):
   the sound of wind blowing through trees
   the sound of glass breaking
   the sound of a typewriter in action
   the sound of a person walking through mud
   the sound of a thunderstorm
   (from *New Directions in Creativity*)

3. Complete the phrases below with a "word–picture" that makes an original and appropriate response:
   as funny as...
   as quick as...
   as frightened as...
   as nervous as...
   as tired as...

4. What colors do you see when you think of the following: each day of the week, each month of the year, the seasons?
   What do the following colors make you think of: red, blue, brown, yellow, black, green, white, orange, pink?

5. Answer each of the following questions and give a reason for your response.

What does laughter taste like?
Which is itchier, a wool sweater or curiosity?
What color is noise?
Which is slower, K or Z?
(from *Write Now*)

Several more examples of the above kinds of questions can be found in many of the resources listed at the end of this article. Encourage students to make up their own questions, and to try them out on their classmates.

The ability to engage in creative thinking is a vital part of the early stages of any writing effort. Ideas must be generated, modified, and shaped to suit one's purpose and audience, and this process, moreover, should be done in an atmosphere free of premature evaluation, either from oneself or from others. The skills and attitude involved in creative thinking, once developed, will serve students well as a tool to bring about mastery of, and satisfaction with, the basic communication skills that they will encounter in future language arts classes.

References

Dodd, Anne Wescott. *Write Now!: Insights Into Creative Writing*. New York: Learning Trends, 1973.

Laliberte, Norman, and Kehl, Richey. *100 Ways to Have Fun With an Alligator & 100 Other Involving Art Projects*. Blauvelt, New York: Art Education, Inc., 1969.

Littell, Joy, and Littell, Joseph Fletcher, eds. *Language of Man* (Book 1). Evanston: McDougal, Littell and Company, 1972.

Renzulli, Joseph S., and Callahan, Carolyn M. *New Directions in Creativity* (Mark B). New York: Harper & Row, Publishers, 1973.

Schrank, Jeffrey. *The Creativity Kit*. (A multi-media learning resource.) Order from The Learning Seed Company, 145 Brentwood Drive, Palatine, Illinois 60067.

Talkers–Coaches–Observers: A Group Discussion Procedure

John Staley, State University of New York at Buffalo

Talkers–Coaches–Observers, a widely used discussion format, is a three-ring procedure. It can be used to structure classroom discussions for maximal use of class time and for total engagement of all class members. Each of the rings has a different role in the discussion group; each provides a different type of involvement in the process. The Talker's role is to discuss the topic in a panel format, speaking freely and reporting in a written statement personal reactions to the discussion group experience. The Coach's role is to observe a Talker and to describe in writing what that Talker contributed to the discussion and how he or she interacted with the other Talkers. By offering helpful suggestions, the Coaches attempt to help the Talkers to improve as discussants and to clarify the effects of their behavior on others in the talking group. The Observer's role is to focus on the interaction in a written statement. All three groups are given worksheets which explain the function of their roles. (See "Description of the Functions of Talkers-Coaches-Observers" at the end of this article.)

Structuring Groups for Talkers–Coaches–Observers

I used Talkers–Coaches–Observers in a class of 30 students, with the class divided into two groups. Group size varied from 10 to 15 students, depending on the number of students present. Each student listed ten topics. These were compiled into one list, ordered from the most suggested to the least suggested topic. The students selected their roles as a Talker, Coach, or Observer, and the topic for discussion. (Participants generally became very interested and enthusiastic.) My role was that of an observer, not a member of the Observers. Occasionally, when asked by the group, I acted as a consultant for specific information. Since the procedure is quite well-defined for all members of the group, I usually tried to observe, *not* participate.

Two sets of written responses to two topics discussed during the six-week summer program follow. The topics are "Abortion: A One or Two Party Decision" and "Cigarette Smoking: Its Effects."

Student-Written Statements for Talkers–Coaches–Observers

Topic: Abortion—A One or Two Party Decision

The Talking Group 1

Dwayne: I did not like the way the topic was talked about.

Dennis: Abortion deals with a woman either having a child or not; it's her decision.

Cathleen: I wish we had more time to talk: I enjoyed it. If you have the sex, suffer the pain. It is up to whoever is involved. You should make sure that you know what it is before you are involved.

Kandee: Abortion depends on the situation and who is involved. It's a matter of being ready for it and the relationship of the two people.

The Coaching Group 1

Terri:
(coached Cathleen) Cathleen has very good points; somewhat quiet. When she did talk, it was pretty good. She only talked when she was asked a question by another talker.

(group reaction: to Cathleen) The group seemed to look over Cathleen because she had little to say.

Sonya:
(coached Kandee) Kandee gave helpful answers, gave good points, and showed good support with the group.

(group reaction: to Kandee) Kandee seemed to be like a leader in the group. She spoke up a lot.

Calvin:
(coached Dennis) Dennis joined the discussion and showed good support.

(group reaction: to Dennis) Dennis was good at one time. Other times, he was just listening to what was being said.

Michelle:
(coached Dwayne) My observee handled the discussion well. I think he had some good arguments. He brought out all the points of the matter that I thought were important.

(group reaction: to Dwayne) He helped the group as a whole by adding some comments that made the conversation more interesting.

The Observing Group 1

Brenda: The men thought it should be a two-party decision and the ladies thought it should be a one party decision. The people in the group spoke about the same. They looked at both sides of the issue.

Perry: The person who spoke the most was Dwayne and the

one who spoke the least was Dennis. The behavior of the group developed into an argument or disagreement. I was only satisfied when the group came to an agreement that a two party (decision) mattered. The behavior that blocked the task was when the group was shouting instead of talking.

Edward: Dawyne was taking the part of a leader and the rest are responding. They are getting deeper into the discussion.

Dennis and Dwayne are having a rap session about abortion.

Dwayne is asking the questions around the group about if a girl got pregnant at the age of 16? Cathy is speaking on abortion taking the child's life.

Then the teacher takes a part in the discussion. Dwayne and the teacher are rapping on it now. The two females in the discussion are going against each other. At the ending they did not have much to say.

Topic: Cigarette Smoking—Its Effects

The Talking Group 2

Calvin: I feel that the discussion we have with the group was true about smoking. People smoke because they want to feel secure.

James: I feel there was not enough participation in the group.

Sonya: The group discussion was not too bad. I think it could have been better.

Brenda: The group was o.k., but it could be better. Some members in the group talked more than others. Others in the group acted shy and didn't speak as much.

The Coaching Group 2

Terri: Brenda did very good talking at times. She had
(coached Brenda)   very good points and defended herself very well. She could have said a little more.

(group reaction: The reaction of the others toward Brenda was like
to Brenda)   looking over her. James asked her a lot of questions and I think that is the only reason she spoke.

Loretta: What my opinion is on what was contributed from
(coached Calvin)   Calvin was that he was a non-smoker. He didn't hang around smokers too long.

(group reaction: He wasn't asked much.
to Calvin)

Dwayne: He was helpful and very direct about the smoker
(coached James)   and non-smoker. He was just about the whole panel.

He was giving facts about why and how people start smoking. I liked the way he flashed over to something else, but it still pertained to smoking.

(group reaction: to James)   Everyone answered his questions.

The Observing Group 2

Michelle: The group handled the topic well. Everyone had their individual ideas. They all made good points. I think there should have been a few more points discussed.

Dennis: Well to get a better view from this topic, I feel that there is a need for more smokers on the panel.

Ruth: I feel that each person in the talking group was very interesting. Each of them said something that I didn't know about cigarettes which I have been smoking for about five years. I think that each person in the talking group said something that everyone should have been listening to. No one in the front of the class acted in a very shy way. A lot of people would get up there and not say anything.

Kandee: The group is not organized; it seems to be blocked by the matter of non-smokers and smokers. James seems to be the leader of the group or a dictator and not working as a member of a group. There is not much discussion among the members of the group. James expresses himself well with the group or adopts to the group. He recognizes everyone's point of view. Brenda seemed to be with the group and Sonya seemed not to be with it.

The discussion of the topic "Abortion: A One or Two Party Decision" was productive in revealing the discord on the issue. The group tended to polarize, with the females favoring a one party decision and the males a two party decision. The major part of the session reflected the Newman-Oliver discussion objectives of Transmitting Information and Social Opining or Unloading. One of the Talkers dominated the session (as teller) until he voiced a personal opinion that conflicted with another Talker's opinion. Then the discussion would focus on the conflict of opinions. Coaches' comments about the panel's reaction to their Talkers, and Observers' comments on group interaction pointed up specific problem areas.

The topic "Cigarette Smoking—Its Effects" presented a discussion covering three objectives: Transferring Information, Social Opining, and Problem-Solving and Clarification. Again, a dominant Talker emerged, but he stated factual information about the effects of smoking and some statements of Social Opining. Other Talkers affirmed the dominant Talker's statements and offered their opinions on smoking. Within the group, general opinions contrasted nonsmokers' attitudes about smokers and the rights of nonsmokers in the public domain. For periods in the talk, Problem-Solving and Clarification was shown in the group's effort to delineate the clash of smokers' and nonsmokers' public rights.

With the shift of discussion objectives from Transferring Information to Social Opining to Problem-Solving and Clarification, some of the Observers did not perceive the discussion as effective or productive. One Observer felt the discussion needed more smokers on the panel. Another Observer stated the smoker and nonsmoker issue was a block in the discussion process and the process itself was unorganized. However, other Observers found the discussion effective. The shifts of objectives and the Observers' responses presented a good profile of how unsettled the public issue of cigarette smoking still is and how discussions of the issue can falter.

With use of the Talkers–Coaches–Observers procedure, my class came to understand how a discussion group can interact productively or unproductively. The availability of the written statements composed during and immediately after the talk allowed us to review closely the blocks to effective discussion, as well as specific strong areas. Talkers were able to benefit from the comments of their Coaches; Coaches and Observers learned to use both a critical eye and ear to analyze and to articulate the interaction of a discussion group. In addition, the students worked on a basic aspect of writing, simple observing and reporting, and they learned a way to sharpen and improve the focus of written statements.

Appendix

Description of the Functions of Talkers–Coaches–Observers *

Group A: The Talking Group

You will be given a discussion task or topic by your teacher and you will then spend a short period of time talking to others in

---

*Adapted from Alfred H. Gorman, *Teachers and Learners*. Boston: Allyn and Bacon, Inc., 1969.

your group. Listen attentively. Talk when you feel like it. Don't be shy about speaking up. Try to do your part to make it a good discussion.

The teacher will not join in the discussion. There is no group discussion leader.

Your name _____

Your reactions to the discussion experience with your group:

Group B: The Coaching Group

Your name _____

The person you observed _____

During the discussion you will be observing a member of the discussion group. After the discussion you will *describe* for him what he did and offer him *helpful suggestions* about improving himself as a discussant.

Your task is to help the discussant see for himself what kind of contribution he made to the group discussion.

Attempt, below, to describe your observee's behavior in the group. Was he quiet, domineering, helpful to others? Did he support and/or clarify the contributions of others? Did he help the group to formulate its goals? [Leave space.]

Attempt, below, to report, as you saw it, the effects of your observee's behavior on the other members of the group. Did they react, and if so, what were the reactions?

Group C: The Observing Group

Your name _____

You will focus on the interaction of the whole group rather than on the behavior of a specific participant. Following the interaction session, you will have opportunity to compare your findings with those of others in your group.

You will want to note who speaks most and least, who the leaders of the group appear to be, what behaviors seem to produce group action and satisfaction, what behaviors seem to block the group in getting at its task, and whether the group acts as an entire group, as a collection of subgroups, or as an assortment of individuals.

Make your notes below. Specific quotes of significant speeches are helpful.

6 About Teaching Response to Literature and Film

When we begin a unit or course on literature, there is so much we want to teach and share with our students. But one teacher discovered that in order to teach the most about poetry, he had to share literary disasters. Analyzing poems of questionable merit sharpened students' skills in criticism and promoted an appreciation of great literature. Another teacher uses *The Odyssey* to illustrate the three levels of literature: the author's literal, the universal, and the reader's experiential. Film is also a form of literature, as students discover when they learn to study characterization by paying attention to detail, with the help of the Ego States Checklist.

Teaching literature can be very satisfying when you see students begin to analyze, criticize, and appreciate works of art. The ideas offered here have helped students discover literature—and maybe something about themselves.

Uncloistered Is Beautiful

Fred Gilliard, Idaho State University

Rare is the compiler who chooses to feature a bad poem in an anthology; publishers normally desire significant works in their publications. The resounding principle appears to be that students clearly learn more from masterpieces than from lesser works. Unfortunately, continuous reading of and writing about established poems may hamper students' development in that their critical responses become devoid of originality and concreteness—two qualities basic to successful writing.

To promote fresh responses to readings and to emphasize the importance of concreteness in writing, I have designed assignments that require students to grapple with literary disasters. My departure from the virtuous study of cloistered literature is founded on the premise that students can develop critical skills as readily by negative experiences with literature as by positive ones.

I've often used the following poem* as part of a comparison-contrast essay that asks students to evaluate particularly the poem's ideas and images. Usually I juxtapose this poem against one of better quality but on the same general topic.

Pray in May

Today the birds are singing and
The grass and leaves are green,
And all the gentle earth presents
A bright and sunny scene.
It is the merry month of May
When flowers bloom once more,
And there are hopes and happy dreams
And promises in store.

*Both poems cited in this article appear in Laurence Perrine's *Literature: Structure, Sound, and Sense*, 1970.

What time could be more wisely spent
Than this the first of May
To say that we are thankful for
Our blessings every day?
To give our gratitude to God
In humbleness and prayer
And offer deeds of charity
As incense in the air?
Then let us love our neighbor and
Our rich and fruitful sod,
And let us go to church today
And thank almighty God.

Some students do admire the skating rhythm of the lines as well as the obvious rhyme scheme, and the suggestion to pray impresses them as fit matter for poetry. Others question the poem's value. They object to its vagueness and bromidic message that neither intellectually nor artistically satisfies them; such writers deplore the triteness of veneer images such as " ... the birds are singing and The grass and leaves are green," or "the merry month of May."

My students are not previously informed of the dubious worth of "Pray in May." They make that discovery through an encounter with the poem. Any sweeping critical phrases they have acquired by studying great literature have limited application during their analysis. I require that they substantiate observations with specific illustrations, and if no acceptable correlations exist between generalizations and evidence, they must complete remedial activities. Sometimes I direct them to find a poem (from a series I have collected) with a challenging idea in it. Other times, they may have to revise several images from the poem. As a result of the original assignment and consequent remedial activity, students have an opportunity for an unusual and stimulating classroom experience.

But students are clever. Should the pairing of a weak and strong poem be done frequently, they would soon begin to anticipate my strategy. To offset that anticipation I have occasionally devised writing assignments that utilize "Pray in May" and the following poem. Again, my intent is usually to determine if students can ascertain by comparison and contrast the freshness of the experience recorded in the poem and the concreteness of expressions relating that experience:

The Most Vital Thing in Life

When you feel like saying something
    That you know you will regret,
Or keenly feel an insult
    Not quite easy to forget,
That's the time to curb resentment
    And maintain a mental peace,
For when your mind is tranquil
    All your ill-thoughts simply cease.
It is easy to be angry
    When defrauded or defied,
To be peeved and disappointed
    If your wishes are denied;
But to win a worthwhile battle
    Over selfishness and spite,
You must learn to keep strict silence
    Though you know you're right.

So keep your mental balance
    When confronted by a foe,
Be it enemy in ambush
    Or some danger that you know.
If you are poised and tranquil
    When all around is strife,
Be assured that you have mastered
    The most vital thing in life.

If students have learned anything, they should be able to recognize that both these pieces are literary disasters. Some of them prefer "The Most Vital Thing in Life" because it's not as prayer-like as "Pray in May"; the "advice from a poet" motif also impresses them. But perceptive students question whether or not the pedestrian suggestions about keeping "mental balance" is really the most vital thing in life. When examining the imagery in the poem, other students respond positively to the idea of a battle as a focusing device, and those who can recognize alliteration delight in "maintain a mental," "defrauded or defied," etc. But others point out that the poem is visually hazier than "Pray in May," and that the alliteration is gratuitous rather than genuinely effective.

Students often become defensive about "The Most Vital Thing in Life." Its rhyme, rhythm, and message pursuade them the poem has merit. When my initial assignment fails to demonstrate the shortcomings of the selection, I try another tactic. I insert lines or verse paragraphs from it into another poem. By requiring students to ferret out what doesn't belong in the revised work, I afford them another opportunity to reevaluate the effectiveness of the ideas and images in "The Most Vital Thing in Life." This strategy usually succeeds, and not just because the lines or passages are obviously out of place because I make an honest effort to match the inserted lines with an appropriate piece.

Innumerable ways exist for utilizing literary disasters as part of the teaching-learning process. And the basic skills that can be realized from such classroom exercises are not confined to what has been suggested here. No doubt the use of literary disasters will not, and should not, replace the study of masterpieces. Yet an acquaintance with lesser works cannot help but stimulate an appreciation of what is great literature—thereby giving students yardsticks with which to measure their cultural heritage and their own work.

Teaching Literature Experientially

John H. Gottcent, Indiana State University at Evansville

One of the biggest advantages to the current reaction against New Criticism is a renewed interest in what I believe has always been the ultimate value of literature: its reflection of the human experience. Without forgetting the best of Formalism, we are now ready to rediscover the message of literature, to see in it those timeless experiences which both concern and transcend individuals and bind the race together. Moreover, I think this approach can and should be taught without reducing classes to formless encounter sessions. I should like to present the basic theory implicit in this "experiential" view of literature, and a pedagogical plan based on it.

The theory is simple: a literary experience involves three levels, the author's literal, the universal, and the reader's experiential. On the literal level we find the language and conventions of the author's time, and the images, details, and hard facts of the world he or she creates. Usually, two things are true. First, this level contains material familiar to the author: Shakespeare's English, Aeschylus' Chorus, Willy Loman's Chevrolet. Second, these same details are often *not* familiar to modern readers. Even in the case of the most obvious exception—contemporary literature—complete reader familiarity may not exist; for example, few admirers of *Slaughterhouse Five* have experienced World War II German bomb shelters. Most of the time a reader, who must begin with the author's literal level, is treading unfamiliar ground.

The universal level of a literary work contains those ideas, experiences, and insights suggested by the literal details, yet not bound, as the latter always are, to a particular time or place. Intangible, these universals are harder to describe, and we usually resort to vague terms suggesting general categories instead of specifically defining them. Thus, in Sophocles' play, Oedipus' detective-like inquiry and its tragic consequences on the literal level suggest some universal insights about self-awareness, and George and Martha's alcohol, verbal battles, and imagined child in *Virginia Woolf* suggest our universal penchant to avoid facing ourselves.

The universal level, of course, often contains a series of sublevels, for a work may suggest several insights simultaneously. But over and above the myriad aspects of this level, two things are always true about it. First, it contains abstractions which have no tangible existence in themselves and therefore are unfamiliar to *both* author and reader (i.e., neither Sophocles nor ourselves can be said to *know* self-awareness as a thing in itself). Second, the universals are illustrated in—indeed, have an ambient relationship with—*two* sets of details: those the author has selected for the literal level, and those familiar to the reader from personal experience. The reader's job, then, is to discover the universals suggested by the literal details of the work, and to re-illustrate them in terms of a personal experiential level. A student may find in Oedipus' self-realization, for example, an agonizing parallel to her own growing awareness that she is in school for the wrong reasons (to please parents, perhaps) and has embarked on a career without really knowing herself—in fact, Oedipus' story may direct her to this personal insight.

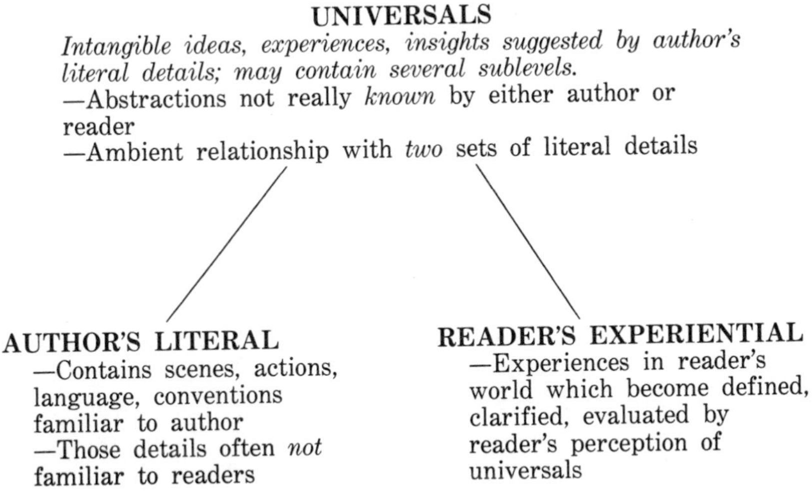

UNIVERSALS

Intangible ideas, experiences, insights suggested by author's literal details; may contain several sublevels.
—Abstractions not really *known* by either author or reader
—Ambient relationship with *two* sets of literal details

AUTHOR'S LITERAL
—Contains scenes, actions, language, conventions familiar to author
—Those details often *not* familiar to readers

READER'S EXPERIENTIAL
—Experiences in reader's world which become defined, clarified, evaluated by reader's perception of universals

Fig. 1. The three levels of literature.

Being aware of these three levels of literary experience and learning to understand them are the goals of a three-stage classroom process: Backgrounds (comprehending the details comprising the author's literal level), Reading (perceiving the universals, but realizing one cannot *know* them), and Response (seeing the connection between the universals and personal experience). I'm going to illustrate this process—and, by implication, the theory underlying it—using *The Odyssey* as an example. Obviously a work this vast is multi-faceted, so I will focus on one question: what can this poem tell us about images of masculinity? We begin with Backgrounds. There is argument over how much background is really necessary to an understanding of this work— some would precede the poem with a mini-course in Greek history; others would begin *in medias res* with no background at all. How much material is necessary can best be answered by remembering the point of all this: to give the student the requisite information for understanding the author's literal level.

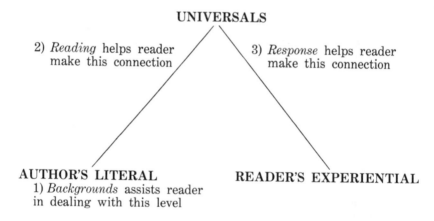

Fig. 2. The three stages of the Experiential Method.

The translator has begun this process by "explaining" Homer's language; an editor may have supplied additional information through an introduction and notes. The teacher begins from here. Students should be made aware of Odysseus' place in Greek mythology and of the Trojan War legends which provide the poem's context. Also, since we plan to deal specifically with Odysseus as man, it might be interesting—though not essential— to discuss the possible historicity of the character. I have found the film "Search for Ulysses," based on Ernle Bradford's attempts to retrace the journey of Odysseus across the Mediterranean, a fascinating speculation which helps generate student interest and also shows them the physical world of Homer's drama. After seeing it, they are better prepared to realize the impact of the story Homer tells.

In stage two, Reading, I try to get my students to recognize some of the ways we can read character in literature. In so doing, they begin to see how the details of Homer's literal level suggest the universals of Odysseus' human personality. One method that has worked particularly well is comparison: we investigate a literary figure by comparing him or her to another person—real or imaginary—whom we already know. In the case of Odysseus I begin by asking what it means, in our society, to be a man. We then formulate a tentative description of the modern American concept of manhood: courage, toughness, cleverness, an interest in sports and cars, the ability to hide emotions (especially not to cry), the ability to remain aloof from emotional entanglements (the *Playboy* image of the man who enjoys women but never "gets involved").

Having constructed this imaginary composite, we next turn to *The Odyssey* to see how many of the traits we have listed also characterize Odysseus. To no one's surprise, we find the Greek hero possesses courage, toughness, and cleverness (the account of his outwitting the Cyclops through the name "Nobody" is particularly applicable here). The next trait, however, may provide a stumbling block: clearly Odysseus has nothing to do with cars or football—but he is adept at the sports of his day (note his prowess in the bow-stringing contest) and at warfare. In short, his interests are traditional manly subjects. In discovering this the students begin to see that they cannot stop at the absence of twentieth-century sports in the poem; they must accept Homer's own details and see behind them an image of masculinity illustrated by different details in our day.

The last two traits are especially revealing. Students are always amazed to find that the obviously masculine Odysseus has no shame about crying. In fact, in his very first appearance (Book V) we find him bawling on the rocks of Calypso's island prison, yearning for home. Later, he will cry openly when reunited with his son, and then his wife. Also, we find that while he does some sleeping around (at least with Circe and Calypso), Odysseus is no playboy. His relationship with Penelope is obviously of prime importance to him (he struggles for ten years to return to her), and he is not afraid to show his emotional involvement; their reunion in Book XXIII is one of the most touching scenes in literature. In these two instances, students see marked differences between Odysseus and contemporary images of maleness.

Having gone through Background and Reading, the students are now ready for the most challenging stage, Response. Ultimately, this must be a personal experience, often gone through outside the classroom—perhaps long after the course is over. But some things can be done in class to help. Discussion of the contrasting images of masculinity, or some pointed comments by the instructor, are good. One device I've found particularly helpful is the journal. I ask my students to write freely, for ten minutes, about their responses to the reading or class discussion. Their comments are never graded, though I do read them and occasionally write reactions. The only requirement is that they write continuously for the ten minutes, usually filling close to one side of a page. Here are samples:

> Being a man—a challenge now as in Odysseus' day. The need to prove oneself—it can be frightening. Poor Telemachos: not only having to be a "man" himself but having to live in the shadow of a famous father—the children of the well-known must bear a double-burden. Yet Odysseus could cry—he had that outlet at least. The wine dark sea—it's kind of eerie to think about it—3,000 years ago the man may have been real, and we can still feel his presence through the book today.

The passage rambles. Nothing is even close to profound. Yet there is at least one new insight, about Telemachos, that never came out in class. And more important, the student is beginning to realize that the fright one feels in trying to live up to a sexual code is something peope have felt for thousands of years.

Other entries show similar insights. The journal forces the student to respond personally to the literature, to begin to see that crying is not necessarily unmasculine, that there can be other dimensions to maleness. She begins, slowly and haltingly, to reevaluate her own, half-conscious definition of manhood, to redefine her relationships to males. She is starting to make the connection between her own experience—the reader's level—and the universals suggested by Homer's literal level. She is learning to read literature.

None of the stages in this process—Backgrounds, Reading, Response—is new. What is important in this back-to-basics era is that we remember their purpose.

The Ego States Checklist: A Basic Approach to Film Characterization

Thomas G. MacLennan, State University of New York at
    Buffalo
Darleen Michalak, State University of New York at Buffalo

Many of the liveliest discussions in English class revolve around student response to the marked increase in characterization in recent feature films. A crucial problem facing any teacher dealing with a discussion of characters in a film is the lack of a *characterization vocabulary* that can be shared by an entire class. E. M. Forster's (1927) "round" and "flat" characterization scheme is helpful; however, student response, even to the more fully "round" film characters, may often be limited by the nature of that media. In another article that dealt with short fiction (Michalak/MacLennan, 1976), we made a distinction between what a character says and does (*exterior* characteristics) and what a character thinks and feels (*interior* characteristics). A skillful short story writer develops a character by employing both of these aspects of characterization. The majority of films seem much more dependent upon developing a character primarily through exterior characteristics. We may see a film character thinking, but, unless a technique such as voice-over-soundtrack narration is employed, we cannot share in that character's thinking processes. In most recent feature films we are left to infer interior characteristics from a character's overt behavior. It seems to us that a major problem in establishing a film characterization vocabulary is in introducing a frame of reference that, while being limited primarily to overt character behavior, is still dynamic enough to reflect change.

We find that when we are viewing a film rich in characterization, rather than following with a general, open-ended class discussion, an *intermediary step* is necessary. We have students complete a dichotomous checklist that enumerates a wide range of character traits, and is designed to reflect the kinds of overt change a character might undergo during the course of a film.

The Ego States Concept

The checklist is based on the concept of ego states, developed by Eric Berne (1964) and elaborated upon by Harris (1969), James and Jongeward (1971), and others. The basic idea is that the behavior of individuals in dealing with other individuals can be categorized as Parent behavior, Adult behavior, and Child behavior. In other articles we have shown how the ego states concept can be employed in the reading and discussion of a short piece of fiction (Michalak/MacLennan, 1976) and in reading and discussing dramatic literature (MacLennan/Michalak, 1976). Since both articles contain ways of introducing the concept in the classroom, we will not elaborate here. Briefly stated, the concept proposes that the Parent ego state contains the attitudes and behavior incorporated from external sources, primarily parents. The Adult ego state is oriented to current reality and the objective gathering of data. The Child ego state contains all the impulses that come naturally to an infant. The checklist is designed so that what Transactional Analysis (TA) proponents would call Parent ego state behavior is represented in questions 1–10, Adult ego state behavior in questions 11–20, and Child ego state behavior in questions 21–30.

The Ego States Checklist

Directions: Place a check in the column labelled YES if you think the questions appropriately describe ___(insert character's name)___. Place a check in the column labelled NO if you think it is not appropriate, or doesn't adequately describe the character. We have included several YES/NO columns in case you want to examine change or lack of change in one character at different points in the film.

	Point in film					
	YES	NO	YES	NO	YES	NO
1. Does the character put words in other character's mouths?						
2. Does (s)he do the thinking for other characters?						
3. Does the character act like (s)he has all the answers?						

4. Does the character frequently offer assistance to others?   ___ ___ ___ ___ ___ ___

5. Does the character try to influence other characters' actions?   ___ ___ ___ ___ ___ ___

6. Does the character frequently protect others?   ___ ___ ___ ___ ___ ___

7. Would the character come to the rescue of others?   ___ ___ ___ ___ ___ ___

8. Is the character's conversation filled with words like "should," "ought," or "must"?   ___ ___ ___ ___ ___ ___

9. Does (s)he treat other characters as inferiors?   ___ ___ ___ ___ ___ ___

10. Is the character's conversation filled with clichés?   ___ ___ ___ ___ ___ ___

11. Is the character a joyless individual?   ___ ___ ___ ___ ___ ___

12. Does the character tend to be like a computer just grinding out information and decisions?   ___ ___ ___ ___ ___ ___

13. Does the character always consider work before pleasure?   ___ ___ ___ ___ ___ ___

14. Is (s)he always rational rather than impulsive in most interactions with others?   ___ ___ ___ ___ ___ ___

15. Does the character always try to reasonably justify his/her behavior?   ___ ___ ___ ___ ___ ___

16. Does the character consider different options before taking action?   ___ ___ ___ ___ ___ ___

17. Does the character appear to be a careful thinker?   ___ ___ ___ ___ ___ ___

18. Would the character refrain from emotional involvement?   ___ ___ ___ ___ ___ ___

19. Would the character's conversation include phrases such as, "Let's be objective" or "What are my options?"   ___ ___ ___ ___ ___ ___

20. Would the character be organized?   ___ ___ ___ ___ ___ ___

21. Does the character surrender authority to others?   ___ ___ ___ ___ ___ ___

22. Does the character enjoy being playful? __ __ __ __ __ __

23. Is the character the type you would be able to have fun with? __ __ __ __ __ __

24. Does (s)he depend too much on others' advice before arriving at a decision? __ __ __ __ __ __

25. Does (s)he tend to look to others for constant approval? __ __ __ __ __ __

26. Does (s)he tend to look to others for support? __ __ __ __ __ __

27. Does (s)he have trouble being self-critical? __ __ __ __ __ __

28. Would you describe this character as being creative? __ __ __ __ __ __

29. Does the character enjoy being pampered? __ __ __ __ __ __

30. Would the character's conversation include such phrases as, "I can't," "Help me," "I won't," or "I don't want to"? __ __ __ __ __ __

Implications for Instruction

Our concern with the lack of an adequate film characterization vocabulary is quite similar to a concern expressed about student writing by Edward B. Jenkinson and Donald A. Seybold in *Writing as a Process of Discovery* (1970). They point out that: "The verb in the instruction is always the same—*write* . . . . If he does not understand the process and if he is not certain what writing is, how can he be expected to write?" All too often we assume students have a characterization frame of reference, that we can apply a similar instructional verb—*talk*, and that fruitful class discussion will automatically follow. It has been our experience that the checklist provides an important and necessary intermediary step that serves as a catalyst for class discussion. For that reason, each one of the thirty statements in our checklist is a very general character trait. Definition refinement will occur during class discussion.

A little earlier, we spoke about the problems of stereotyping. the tri-partite division (Parent, 1–10; Adult, 11–20; Child, 21–30) is an advantage, since a majority of checks in any one subdivision would suggest a stereotyped character. For example, if the check-list were used to elicit student responses to television series characters, most YES responses to Archie Bunker would occur in the first ten questions. If it were used with Mr. Spock ("Star Trek") the majority of YES responses would appear in the middle ten questions. Finally, if it were used to describe Gilligan ("Gilligan's Island") the majority of YES responses would occur in the final ten questions. These general observations can easily lead into class discussion of how and why a character becomes stereotyped.

The checklist's major advantage is that it illustrates *change* in a character's overt behavior during a film, as well as a lack of change. For that reason, we have designed it so that students are able to make a side-by-side general comparison of one character's behavior at different points in the film. A recent film character that undergoes a major transformation is Adrian, the girlfriend in *Rocky*. Each section of the checklist helps direct class discussion toward overt changes in Adrian's behavior at two points in the film: prior to dating Rocky and after dating Rocky.

She seems less prone to think for other characters (#2), and less anxious to influence the actions of her brother, Paulie (#5), after she begins dating Rocky. These general observations could easily lead to class discussion concerning the change in her relationship with Paulie during the course of the film.

The checklist responses might also indicate that she *was* a joyless individual prior to dating Rocky (#11). After dating Rocky she begins to indulge in emotional involvement and impulsiveness (#18). Her tendency to reject all emotion in her dealings with others (#14) is curbed. Class discussion, stimulated by the general terminology, would refine these general observations and elicit other viewpoints.

The final ten questions could promote student discussion of what may be the most dramatic overt changes in Adrian. She is less likely to surrender authority to others (#21), most noticeably her brother, Paulie. Adrian seems much more assertive and less prone to seek approval and depend on others' advice (#24–27). Once again, class discussion might challenge any of these perceived changes, or lead to some broader questions. What kind of credibility problems does the radical transformation Adrian undergoes during the film cause a viewer? What might be some objections of the characterizations of Adrian from a feminist's viewpoint?

Since the *time factor* is important, we ask students to complete the checklist as soon as possible after viewing a film. A major purpose of the checklist is to aid students in organizing their general responses to a character prior to class discussion. We have also found the checklist helpful when texts are not available, since the general nature of the checklist may remind a student of a key scene or an important transitional scene in a film.

We see the checklist as being valuable in the same way Young, Becker & Pike (1970) claim a heuristic procedure is helpful; it may help a student remember what (s)he already knows about a character, it may draw student attention to aspects of a character that may have been initially overlooked, and—when supplemented by class discussion—it can be helpful in organizing a student's general response to a film character by supplying a dynamic frame of reference.

References

Berne, Eric. *Games People Play: The Psychology of Human Relationships.* New York: Grove Press, 1964.

Forster, E. M. *Aspects of the Novel.* New York: Harcourt Brace Jovanovich, Inc., 1947.

Harris, Thomas A. *I'm OK—You're OK: A Practical Guide to Transactional Analysis.* New York: Harper & Row, 1969.

James, Muriel, and Jongeward, Dorothy. *Born to Win: Transactional Analysis with Gestalt Experiments.* Reading, Mass.: Addison–Wesley, 1971.

Jenkinson, Edward B., and Seybold, Donald A. *Writing As a Process of Discovery: Some Structured Theme Assignments for Grades Five through Twelve.* Bloomington, Ind.: Indiana University Press, 1970.

MacLennan, Thomas G., and Michalak, Darleen. "Non-verbal Communication in Drama." In *Creative Dramatics in the Language Arts Classroom,* edited by Patrick J. Finn and Walter T. Petty. Report of the Second Annual Conference on Language Arts at State University of New York at Buffalo, 1976.

Michalak, Darleen, and MacLennan, Thomas G. "Transactional Analysis and Characterization in Fiction." *The English Record* 27: 60–68.

Young, Richard E.; Becker, Alton L.; and Pike, Kenneth L. *Rhetoric: Discovery and Change.* New York: Harcourt, Brace & World, Inc., 1970.